the RACE
trap

Smart Strategies for
EFFECTIVE RACIAL
COMMUNICATION
in Business and in Life

the RACE *trap*

Dr. ROBERT L. JOHNSON
& Dr. STEVEN SIMRING

with Gene Busnar

HarperBusiness
An Imprint of HarperCollins*Publishers*

HarperCollins books may be purchased for educational, business, or sales promotional use. For information please write: Special Markets Department, HarperCollins Publishers Inc., 10 East 53rd Street, New York, NY 10022.

FIRST EDITION

Designed by William Ruoto

Printed on acid-free paper

Library of Congress Cataloging-in-Publication Data

Johnson, Robert L.
   The race trap : smart strategies for effective racial communication in business and in life / Robert L. Johnson and Steven Simring with Gene Busnar.—1st ed.
      p. cm
   ISBN 0-06-662001-5 (hc)
   1. Intercultural communication—United States.   2. Communication and culture—United States.   3. United States—Race relations.   4. Whites—United States—Communications.   5. Afro-Americans—Communication.   I. Simring, Steven. II. Busnar, Gene.   III. Title.
HM1211.J64   2000
303.48'2'0973—dc21   00-038327

00 01 02 03 04 ❖/RRD 10 9 8 7 6 5 4 3 2 1

*To Maxine, Susie, Liz, and all
the kids—especially Nadine*

Contents

Acknowledgments

The concept of a book about smart racial communication first came from the very special literary agents, Herb and Nancy Katz. They took the idea as far as they could; then, with enormous grace and generosity, turned the project over to us to develop on our own.

Hundreds of friends, students, colleagues, and even perfect strangers responded to our surveys. At last, we obtained the hard data we needed to write a book. Even if we had the space, we could not thank each of our respondents by name because we promised anonymity. Jamie Forbes gave us invaluable feedback on the manuscript and expert editing on the proposal and the original drafts. Rosa Godwin and Keith Bratcher are our right and left arms, without whom we could never get anything accomplished.

An idea is just an idea until someone comes along to position it, package it, and sell it. Linda Konner is our tough, outspoken, endlessly creative agent, who recognized the urgent need for effective racial communication in business. She helped us refocus our concept, and then introduced us to Dave Conti, our editor at HarperBusiness. Dave's support and guidance have been invaluable. The whole staff at Harper has been great, including Lisa Berkowitz, publicist *extraordinaire,* her associate Michele Jacob, and the highly talented art director, Roberto de Vicq.

Our wonderful families were always there to help us and cheer us on. The spirit of Minnie Klavans looks down and guides us all.

Introduction

We met in 1976, shortly after both of us joined the faculty at New Jersey Medical School in Newark. Here was an institution built from the ashes of that city's 1967 race riots. Some still argue that those riots were sparked by the state's plans to launch a new health sciences university on a large tract of land in the middle of a decaying, primarily black inner city.

The politicians and health care administrators thought they were bringing a precious gift to the community. But the ensuing violence demonstrated that many of Newark's black residents held a radically different view.

When the smoke finally cleared, representatives of the state sat down with community leaders to design a scaled-back hospital and medical school complex. The community demanded that racial preferences be given at all levels of the institution, from senior faculty and top administrators down to housekeeping staff. The school set aside 25 percent of its slots for minority medical students—giving it one of the highest black enrollments of any American medical school.

We were both active participants in these painful battles, and there were times we were on opposite sides of the fence. Still, we were always able to agree on at least one major point:

When it comes to race relations, the real battleground is personal—not political.

This fundamental agreement led to an ongoing dialogue about the difficulties blacks and whites have interacting with one another—particularly in workplace and business situations. We reviewed as many books and articles on the subject of race as we could find. It seemed to us that almost all of these authors were missing the mark.

When intellectuals get into debates about affirmative action and the politics of race, they are usually talking about things that have little or no impact on most people's day-to-day lives. It struck us that the most important questions have to do with the things that happen to real people every day—on the job, on the street, in school, and in doctors' offices.

It was clear that trying to alter people's racial biases is next to impossible, at least in the short run. Instead, we decided to develop a program to help individuals of different races have more productive negotiations and avoid getting caught in a variety of what we call "race traps." We discovered that the best way for women and men to accomplish this is to become more racially intelligent.

From the outset, we recognized that people were most concerned about better racial communications in business and the workplace. This is the domain where individuals earn their livelihood, and the place they are most likely to come in contact with members of different groups. So, it's not surprising that the vast majority of our respondents feel that this is where they have most at stake. Accordingly, most of our attention is devoted to business. Still, we have found that racial intelligence cannot be compartmentalized.

Men and women who can effectively communicate with people of other races in a business situation can transfer those skills to their dealings with cops, judges, doctors, clerks, and anyone they may encounter on the street. On the other hand, those who are not smart in dealing with bank tellers, waiters, or teachers of other races are likely to behave similarly in a work environment.

This book deals primarily with issues involving blacks and whites. However, its principles are equally relevant to members of all racial and ethnic groups. The chapters that follow will help both white readers and nonwhite readers who want to get ahead without getting tripped up by racial conflicts.

WHO NEEDS THIS BOOK?

- Corporate leaders and diversity managers.
- Sales and customer service professionals.

- Entrepreneurs.
- Supervisors and employees in a racially diverse workplace.
- Job seekers and college applicants.
- Educators, school administrators, and students.
- Readers who are obliged to deal with police, doctors, or teachers.
- Readers who want to receive better service in their daily dealings.

THE RESEARCH

The suggestions and conclusions presented in the following chapters are informed by over forty years of collective clinical experience and four years of case-study research. As part of this project, we developed the Racial Intelligence Quotient (RQ), and tested it for validity with focus groups of men and women from a broad range of racial, ethnic, and socioeconomic backgrounds.

Our case studies were collected through personal interviews and surveys that were conducted over the Internet. Detailed analyses of 250 of these cases were used to illustrate key points and concepts throughout the book; they form the basis for the tests we ask you to take in Chapters Two and Eleven.

THE CHAPTERS

In Chapter One, we explore how becoming racially smarter can help you avoid race traps in business and everyday life. We describe some of the common problems blacks and whites have with one another, and discuss why it's essential never to discount race in any diversity encounter.

In Chapter Two, we ask you to complete the RQ Test. As you go through the questions, don't worry about which choice is politically correct. Instead, put yourself in the place of the person confronting each situation, and select the answer that you believe most furthers your interests.

Chapter Three describes the eight-step process we have developed for communicating more effectively across racial lines. In

Chapter Four, we explore the language of race, and discuss the differences between overt, covert, and accidental racism.

In Chapter Five, we develop common principles for helping organizations, managers, and workers avoid getting caught in race traps. In Chapters Six, Seven, and Eight, we show you how to apply the tenets of effective racial communication to sales and customer service, the system, and daily life.

In Chapter Nine, we ask you to score the RQ Test, and to consider why some responses make more sense than others in negotiating diversity encounters.

In Chapter Ten, we show you how to apply the same eight-step process to help your children become more effective in their racial dealings.

Chapter Eleven contains a series of follow-up questions designed to help you analyze and apply the key concepts we explore in the book to real-life situations.

As physicians, we are committed to the belief that problems are much more easily prevented than cured. We find this principle to be equally pertinent to our corporate and business-consulting work. We wrote this book to help you deal better with people of other races—and to avoid trouble. Once you get the basics down, we believe you will become a better manager, a more effective salesperson, a more upwardly mobile employee, and a more desirable job applicant.

Please keep in mind that we have no interest in convincing people to alter their views—only their behaviors. Our research has taught us that being a liberal, a conservative—or even a bigot—does not accurately predict a person's racial intelligence.

If reading these chapters can help some readers become more accepting of racially different people, that would be great. But our primary commitment is simply this: to show you how to have more effective dealings with people of different racial groups—be they bosses, customers, coworkers, employees, or others you encounter in conducting life's business.

We dedicate our book to that purpose.

ONE

BECOMING A SMART
RACIAL COMMUNICATOR

Genius may have its limitations, but stupidity is not thus handicapped.
—ELBERT HUBBARD

Hardly a day passes when some aspect of the race debate is not in the headlines. Whatever our business or profession and wherever we operate geographically, race is an issue for all of us.

- If you're not white, you probably don't need to be reminded of the impact race has on your life. Chances are, many of those who affect your day-to-day existence—teachers, cops, lawyers, doctors, employers—have always been white. For better or worse, people often make judgments on the basis of skin color—judgments that don't always work in your favor. Which is why, when blacks wake up in the morning, they are more likely to have race on their minds than whites. Still, race is something nobody can afford to ignore.
- If you're white, you are far more likely to come in contact with people of different racial and ethnic groups than before—both in the workplace and in everyday life.

In a corporate setting, the chances of having coworkers, supervisors, and customers who are African American, Hispanic, or Asian are almost double what they were ten years ago. The cop who pulls you over on the highway is also more likely to be black or Latino. So is the doctor who examines you at a hospital or managed-care facility.

Whatever your race or ethnicity, the way you handle interactions with people of other races will have an impact on your career, your health and well-being, and the ease with which you negotiate your day-to-day transactions in the world at large. In this book, we refer to such interactions as "diversity encounters."

Intellectuals and politicians have provided an almost endless stream of rhetoric about affirmative action, racial tensions, white racism, black racism—not to mention playing the so-called race card. Virtually all of these commentators have a philosophical, political, legal, or social ax to grind. We won't be engaging in any of these self-serving, unresolvable arguments. They have no bearing on racial intelligence.

In our research, we have analyzed some 250 case studies about diversity encounters. We have developed an objective measurement called the Racial Intelligence Quotient (RQ), which measures an individual's level of skill in dealing with members of other racial groups.

The RQ has little, if anything, to do with morality or higher ethical concepts. For example, a person can have a high RQ, even if he or she harbors personal bias or negative attitudes. While we haven't come across any Klansmen or neo-Nazis with high RQs, we found that there was little difference between liberals and conservatives when it comes to being racially intelligent.

This book will help you raise your RQ, and while you do this, you will become more effective in negotiating the delicate, often tricky, racial terrain. As you become more racially smart, you will be better able to negotiate interactions in ways that maximize your self-interest. This process doesn't happen overnight. But fortunately, it doesn't take long to achieve a small but significant improvement in racial intelligence—and small improvements make a big difference in what happens in five critical domains.

FIVE CRITICAL AREAS FOR EFFECTIVE RACIAL COMMUNICATION

1. *The workplace*: Getting along with coworkers, colleagues, supervisors, and employees.

2. *Sales and customer service*: Marketing your product to a diverse consumer base. Closing the deal.

3. *The system*: Dealing with police officers, judges, doctors, teachers, bureaucrats, and others in a position to make your (or your child's) life miserable.

4. *Daily life*: Receiving good service in stores, restaurants, banks, and airports.

5. *Child rearing*: Helping children become more effective in maintaining good relationships with teachers, classmates, and friends of different racial groups.

While our primary focus is business and the workplace, it's important to keep in mind that the business we transact in our dealings with the system and in daily life are no less critical to our success and well-being. If you're racially smart at an airport or in a doctor's office, you're likely to carry those skills into the workplace, and vice versa.

This is not a book on parenting. Nevertheless, we show parents how to teach their children to navigate diversity encounters—not just because it's the warm and fuzzy or politically correct thing to do. We see racial intelligence as a critical evolutionary step, one that will continue to exert an ever greater influence on the success of these emerging citizens in the future.

RACIAL INTELLIGENCE, IQ, AND COMMON SENSE

Racial intelligence has little to do with a person's overall intelligence. There are men and women with IQs in the so-called genius range who are racially quite stupid. On the other hand, there are many people with modest IQs who are highly effective in negotiating diversity encounters.

No racial group scores better or worse on the RQ Test than any other. The key factors in becoming racially smarter are experience with diversity encounters, motivation, and an ability to separate well-considered objectives from emotional reactions. No other qualifications are needed.

Unlike IQ, which remains relatively consistent over time, a person's RQ is a set of cognitions that constantly changes as it is refined through experience. When you first become aware of the principles of effective racial communication, you may find yourself self-consciously applying them in diversity encounters. But in time, these skills become an automatic part of your operational style.

People with high RQs appear to have a great deal of what is generally referred to as "common sense"—a term that's often used to describe knowledge that is self-evident. Men and women with good common sense can exercise this ability in a wide range of contexts. They are the antithesis of absentminded professors—geniuses in one area, but bumbling fools in other aspects of life.

As we observe the way many people act, and we listen to what they say, it's clear that common sense isn't all that common. Furthermore, even people who appear to possess this quality are often lacking in racial smarts—which turns out to be a type of knowledge that is anything but self-evident. How, then, does one bridge the gap?

You don't need to gather specific information about other cultures—unless you're engaged in some kind of market research. For example, General Motors created a compact car and called it the Chevy Nova. It's unclear if they were interested in selling that product to Spanish-speaking people. But if they were, someone should have noticed that the phrase "*no va*" means "no go" in Spanish—not the brightest name for a car.

Most of us don't need that kind of detailed knowledge or understanding to be racially smart in our normal dealings. For example, it's not necessary for a white person to know a whole lot about the Reverend Martin Luther King Jr. to understand that he is an icon to most black Americans. It's enough to know that when white people discuss Martin King's personal life, question his politics, or debate the appropriateness of creating a holiday in his honor, blacks are likely to interpret that as bias.

Becoming racially smarter is a little like dressing for success. In certain business contexts, for example, it's imperative to dress conservatively. You may prefer wearing jeans and a T-shirt, but you dress in a way that facilitates your goals and avoids making your clothes a distracting side issue.

People sometimes ask: How can you compare something as superficial as how you dress with smart interracial communication?

Again, our concern is facilitating effective interaction—not convincing people to love one another. Perhaps becoming racially smarter will make people more appreciative and accepting of each other's ways. That remains to be seen. The point is that developing a higher RQ is a valuable pursuit on its own terms. It is a key to smoother, more productive dealings between people of different racial and ethnic groups. And it enables people and companies to become more successful.

A person's race may be genetically determined, but racial intelligence is a product of learning and experience. Your RQ responses reflect your views on managing interactions with people of different races—diversity encounters—as well as how you are likely to act in those encounters. These attitudes and behaviors come out of the following environmental inputs:

- Where and when you were born and grew up.
- Your family's racial makeup, and their racial attitudes.
- The people with whom you socialize and form friendships.
- Where you went to school, and your level of education.
- Previous diversity encounters in the workplace.
- Previous diversity encounters in everyday commerce and with the system.
- Attitudes and impressions from the media.

Your brain processes all these data, and what comes out is your *worldview* (how you feel) and your *operational style* (how you act). Your RQ will improve as you become more experienced and more knowledgeable about negotiating diversity encounters.

We have designed the real-life examples on the RQ Test and throughout the chapters to give you a broad range of diversity encounters to handle at your own pace. Think of it as a safe way to add another input to your existing pool of personal skills.

The RQ test is an opportunity to consider various response options in terms of potential consequences—without the emotional pressure of having to negotiate face-to-face situations that, if handled unintelligently, can have serious consequences.

Keep in mind that there is no inherently right or wrong way to feel or behave—at least not from the perspective of racial intelligence. The only way to determine whether a response is racially smart is to ask yourself the following questions:

- Does it make sense?
- Is it helping me become more effective in realizing my goal?

There are all sorts of intense feelings loaded onto the issue of race, which is why people sometimes have trouble accepting this kind of practical approach. Yet, our research clearly demonstrates that the key to becoming racially smarter is to focus on pragmatics. Biases and political opinions matter only to the extent that they have an impact on behavior.

WARNING: DON'T EVER DISCOUNT RACE!

Politicians often talk about creating a race-neutral world. However, no diversity encounter is ever race-neutral—just as no encounter between a man and a woman is ever completely gender-blind. Even when there is no overt friction, there is likely to be a certain amount of latent tension between people of different races—at least in their initial contacts. That's why people tend to be most comfortable with others of their own race and cultural background. But we can't always choose whom we interact with, once we leave our safe, private spaces. Consider these five scenarios:

1. You are a white middle manager, and your black supervisor has been highly critical of work you believe to be excellent.

2. You are a white motorist who has just been pulled over by a black policeman for going five miles above the posted speed limit.

3. You are a black high school graduate about to be interviewed for a high-paying job by the white personnel director of a major corporation. The guidance counselor has suggested that you don't wear your diamond earring at the interview. Your friends say taking it off makes you a sellout.

4. You are a white customer having dinner out with a group of white friends. Your server, who happens to be black, is taking forever to bring your food.

5. You are a black business executive shopping in an upscale department store when you suddenly notice a white security guard monitoring your every move.

A person's racial intelligence will have a significant impact on each of these encounters. Whether that impact is positive or negative depends on one's ability to negotiate effectively. As with all successful negotiations, the first step is knowing what results you want:

1. The white middle manager would like to work without interference from his black supervisor. When evaluation time comes, he wants that supervisor to give him a high performance rating that leads to a hefty raise.

2. The white motorist hopes to come out of the interaction with the black officer without a traffic ticket.

3. The black high school graduate wants the white personnel director to give him that high-paying job, but doesn't want to feel compromised.

4. The white restaurant customer would like the black server to bring his food promptly.

5. The black business executive does not want to be detained and searched by the white security guard.

Good racial intelligence will help generate positive outcomes in all diversity encounters. But remember, there will often be factors that don't involve race. For example, a workplace supervisor may find fault with an employee for any number of reasons. But when two people are of different races, neither one can afford to leave racial differences out of the equation.

People get trapped when they discount or minimize the importance of race. Indeed, racial intelligence is important even when two people of the same race interact.

For example, a black supervisor who chides a black employee might be accused by that employee of trying to curry favor with white higher-ups by being unduly harsh with one of his own. Similarly, a black department store security guard may be carrying out stated or de facto company policy when he scrutinizes the movements of a black customer. Or a white manager may be accused by his white boss of going too easy on his black employees. From this perspective, it always pays to view all interactions—even same-race ones—in a racially sophisticated way.

Some would argue that race shouldn't matter as much as it does. We agree. A person's race *shouldn't* matter! But it does. Our concern is dealing with the world as it is, not how we'd like it to be.

Our research shows that men and women who develop racial-effectiveness skills will encounter significantly fewer problems and have more productive negotiations with people of different racial groups. Consider still another true-life diversity encounter:

A white professor *at a large northeastern medical school loudly criticized her black secretary for distributing the wrong midterm test papers to an auditorium of first-year students.*

"You wouldn't talk that way to me if I were white," the secretary shouted as she walked out of the auditorium. The following week, the secretary filed a hostile workplace lawsuit against the professor and the university.

Now ask yourself the following questions:

- Would the professor have chided a white secretary in the same manner?
- Would the black secretary have been equally offended if the reprimand had come from a black professor?

When a diversity encounter turns into a racially charged event, it becomes next to impossible to answer these questions after the fact. That is why it's important to avoid getting trapped by such incidents—and that means always anticipating the racial component of any black-on-white interaction.

A supervisor or manager ought never to abuse or publicly embarrass any employee. But such indiscretions will rarely lead to a lawsuit—unless the target of the abuse is in a *protected category*— that is, an identifiable minority group whose rights are specifically safeguarded by law. It may not be fair, but employees who are genuinely ill-treated are unlikely to prevail in court unless they can prove that the abuse is based on race, gender, age, disability, or a similar category.

The need to become racially smarter is pragmatic, not idealistic. Keep in mind that our civil rights laws are not designed to protect employees against ordinary mistreatment. During the debate over the 1964 Civil Rights Bill, the late Senator Hubert Humphrey, a leading sponsor of the legislation, noted that the act "does not limit the employer's freedom to hire, fire, promote or demote for any reason—or for no reason—so long as his action is not based on race."[1]

This concept resonates today in a workplace where new discrimination lawsuits are an almost daily occurrence.

In one case that became the subject of a book, an African American attorney named Lawrence Mungin sued his law firm for racial discrimination. According to Mungin, a graduate of Harvard Law School, the firm's partners gave him insulting assignments, left him out of important meetings, and denied him regular contact with clients. After Mungin was not formally evaluated as he was promised, one of the partners told him, "You fell between the cracks."[2]

Lawrence Mungin asserted that the partners saw him as "a racial token" rather than as "a real lawyer." Mungin could point to no racial epithets, or any other specific evidence that he was singled out because of his race. In fact, there were indications that the partners considered a black lawyer from Harvard an asset to their firm. The law firm did not try to prove that it treated Mungin well. Instead, it sought to demonstrate that it treated most of its employees shabbily.

A predominantly black jury awarded Mungin $2.5 million in damages. In civil damages trials, juries are free to do almost anything they want. However, white appeals court judges nullified the jury verdict, and labeled it as unreasonable. The white medical school professor who yelled at her black assistant also claimed that her misbehavior was a function of a "bad temper," and had nothing to do with race. The parties eventually settled out of court, but such cases are always close calls when they go to trial.

Rudeness and a lack of consideration are never advisable—even if they aren't forbidden by law. But when you throw them into a diversity encounter, the mixture can become both incendiary and the basis for legal action. Our focus is to help corporate leaders, managers, and employees on every level prevent seemingly trivial situations from exploding into full-blown disasters.

It makes sense for business leaders to foster a racially smart corporate culture—not just because they are fearful of litigation or want to appear as if they care about the concerns of minorities.

Any company that plans to stay competitive in the coming years must recognize that a racially smart workforce can have a substantial impact on the bottom line.

Entrepreneurs, salespeople, job applicants, and customer service professionals have just as high a stake in becoming racially smarter. An inadvertent word or gesture can turn off a customer or an interviewer, thus causing a substantial financial loss.

Our goal is to help you develop the skills you need to avoid miscommunication and antagonism in a variety of work- and business-related environments.

RACIAL MINORITIES AND THE QUEST FOR POWER

Harvard Business School professor Rosabeth Moss Kantor has observed that, in most American companies, nonwhites "have to do twice as much to get half as far" as their white counterparts."[3]

We are told that by the year 2010, as many as 80 percent of all new entrants to the workforce will be minorities and women. Many companies are adapting to this shifting demographic fact by hiring more people of color. But that doesn't necessarily translate to a significant increase at "the upper ends of professional and managerial pyramids."

A primary reason for this reality is that the power in most American companies is held by white males. Since people tend to be most comfortable with others like themselves, Kantor notes, the white business leader typically shares his power with "someone he can relate to. Someone who reminds him of himself. Someone who looks just like him."

Without the opportunity to attain real power, which she defines as the ability "to participate in decisions, to gain access to resources, information, and political support that ensure that their voices are heard and that they can get things done," Professor Kantor says that "even the most talented people can find themselves stuck in dead-end jobs."

Most nonwhite men and women who achieve career success have become skillful at navigating a world in which whites hold the vast majority of the power positions. This is not to say that these individuals have been compromised or co-opted. As we see it, most of them have found ways to manipulate the system in order to attain a competitive edge. They've accomplished this feat by staying focused on their goals and relegating other issues to the back burner.

In order to be racially smart, you need to recognize what cards you hold in any given situation, and then to play your hand accordingly. All of the African Americans and Latinos we interviewed who've achieved success in corporate America agreed that it is essential to take the initiative, and not expect anything to come without effort.

"You have to take responsibility for your career," says Walter, a senior manager at a top financial institution. "Most white people aren't racists, but they still may be uncomfortable mixing with black and brown coworkers."*

Walter also speaks of how important it is to network with peers, and to find mentors and other powerful people who are in a posi-

---

* To protect the privacy of survey respondents, all names have been changed.

tion to help advance your career. These contacts are often made in social settings, where people tend to seek out others who are like themselves.

Walter observes, for example, that when male executives go out for drinks after work or smoke expensive cigars, women are excluded by the very nature of that bonding. The same kind of thing happens to racial and ethnic minorities—unless a person takes positive action.

"If you want to become part of a particular social circle or activity," Walter told us, "you have to be proactive. Several years ago, a group of managers on my level and higher were organizing a Saturday tennis game. Even though they talked about their plans in my presence, I wasn't invited to play. I wouldn't say it was blatant racism, but it's possible that they assumed that tennis wasn't a sport that black guys play. As it happened, I had been on my college tennis team—but I didn't mention that to my coworkers.

"At first, I allowed the situation to develop—without commenting. Still, I couldn't help but notice that these guys were becoming very close, and I was being left out of this emerging club. I figured that, eventually, this exclusion was going to have a negative impact on my career. So, instead of continuing to sit there passively, I mentioned my experience at tennis, and asked if I could join them.

"A few of the guys seemed surprised, but I was more or less welcomed into the group. I didn't feel especially comfortable about inviting myself, but I know I did the right thing."

Walter adds that the same principle applies to finding mentors: "Corporate cultures are dominated by white males. That's simply a fact of life. Most white males are more comfortable mentoring other white males—which is understandable. Still, if you ask for their help, people usually don't withhold it."

Gary, an African American engineer, observes that white supervisors sometimes walk on eggshells around black employees. "It's hard to get them to give an honest appraisal of your performance—as if you'll interpret a negative evaluation as racism or use it as grounds for a lawsuit."

Gary thought that the most effective way to deal with these suspicions was to let others know, through words and actions, that you value their feedback—negative as well as positive. In general, the best way to take control of that kind of situation is to reframe the issues in a nonthreatening way.

A little humor or a self-deprecating remark is often a useful technique for letting people around you know that you are open to criticism. You may feel as if you're putting yourself on the line by giving others the power to judge you. But what you're actually doing is seizing control of the situation.

TEN COMPLAINTS BLACKS HAVE ABOUT WHITES

1. They don't think we're as smart.
2. They push ahead of us in store and restaurant lines.
3. They inappropriately address us using first names.
4. They can't tell us apart.
5. They attribute our successes to affirmative action.
6. They wrongfully suspect us of criminal behavior—based on racial stereotypes.
7. They consider each of us as representing our race.
8. They're afraid of us, like white taxi drivers who refuse to pick us up.
9. They don't acknowledge past oppression as relevant to current social problems.
10. They underestimate African American cultural contributions.

WHITE ANXIETY OVER LOSING POWER

A good deal has been written about white people (especially males) who are nervous about losing power, as blacks and other minorities continue to enhance their positions in business and society. The effects of this progress have been slow and incremental. Nevertheless, they are impossible to ignore.

Men and women who are confident in their abilities don't fear competition from people of any color. Such fears of losing power bespeak a fundamental insecurity that often has nothing to do with race. If the guy you think is threatening your position looks like you, your fear and anger are likely to be directed just at him, and not to other members of his group.

If, however, your real or perceived competitor is someone of a different color, that negativity can be projected onto an entire race. At that point, it's understandable how such feelings get expressed in racially mindless language and behavior. Understandable, but totally unproductive.

It's true that white males have taken quite a hit over the past few decades. Not long ago, they could call their female coworkers "honey," and pass off sexist remarks as harmless jokes. Blacks and other minorities were often perceived as powerless and invisible. They were treated and talked about disrespectfully, almost as a matter of course. No company would ever officially acknowledge sanctioning such behavior and language, but it was hardly underground.

Corporate diversity programs are often cited as the root cause of white male fears. Such programs are the product of government mandates, as well as marketplace realities. As one senior executive of a Fortune 500 company remarked:

"We commissioned a study to tell us what it would take for us to hold on to the market dominance we have in the New York area. The study said that one of the things we should do is strive to make our managerial workforce look exactly like our customer base." Then she added jokingly, "But this would mean that we wouldn't hire another white male for another fifteen years."[4]

This is no laughing matter for many white males, who feel increasingly resentful and angry over Corporate America's more aggressive diversity programs. In a *Business Week* article entitled "White, Male, and Worried," Laurance Fuller, CEO of Amoco Corporation, was quoted as saying that white males "have nothing to fear but more and better competition. This is to say, then, that some of them have everything to fear."[5]

This kind of economic fear is reminiscent of the pre–Civil Rights South, where poor whites fretted that if blacks were permitted to climb up the economic ladder, they would be relegated to the lowest rung. It found a later expression in the debate over affirmative action, in which whites feared that they would lose out to less-qualified workers strictly on the basis of color. Now it is being voiced as a consequence of the push for diversity.

This argument serves as a handy escape from personal responsibility. All groups have benefited from special advantages in one way or another. If racial minorities are offered certain preferences, it would be senseless for them not to take advantage of those opportunities. If this amounts to playing the race card, then so be it. We all owe it to ourselves to use every advantage at our disposal.

Consider the case of an African American college graduate applying to medical school. The young man graduated number one in his class, and achieved an almost perfect score on his medical boards. In addition, he was extremely personable and well-spoken.

Few school administrators would admit it, but a young man in that position will be courted far more aggressively and offered far more financial perks than, say, a white or Asian student with the identical credentials. Why? Because having a person like that attend your institution is a tremendous public relations coup.

What should you have this young man do? Not to take full advantage of the scholarship offered would signal a complete lack of common sense—not to speak of racial intelligence.

But how would you react if you were a white premed student with identical grades—or a parent of that student? Would you call a right-wing radio talk show and complain that "they" get all the breaks? Or would you pursue your own best opportunity? These are moot questions for the racially smart, whatever their color. The only way to become empowered is to figure out the best way to negotiate the total landscape in front of you.

For most nonwhites, race has always been a key factor—which doesn't necessarily mean that they know how to handle diversity encounters in the most effective way. For white people, the issue of race is becoming an ever more critical part of their day-to-day reality. Tuning out race is dangerous, and complaining about perceived inequities is fruitless. In the final analysis, there really is just one choice: deal with all diversity encounters in the smartest possible way.

TEN COMPLAINTS WHITES HAVE ABOUT BLACKS

1. They attribute all problems to racial prejudice.
2. They expect special consideration and treatment.
3. They think we all look alike.
4. They don't acknowledge that white people have problems too.
5. They continue to use past oppression as an excuse for social problems.
6. They think they have a monopoly on hipness.
7. They talk back to the screen in movie theaters.
8. They don't respect the police.
9. They play the race card at every opportunity.
10. They're not as smart or industrious as whites and Asians.

WHY THE RQ TEST IS IMPORTANT

Racial intelligence is a product of experience; nobody is born with it, and anybody can acquire it. One way to raise your RQ is through trial and error. Mistakes can be valuable learning tools, but certain mistakes can have painful and long-lasting consequences. Therefore, it's far better to demonstrate poor judgment on a test than in a real-world diversity encounter.

We have designed the RQ Test to give you an opportunity to evaluate a variety of diversity encounters in a risk-free context. The test will also help you evaluate your past experiences in the five domains of racial intelligence by providing a framework to help you do the following:

- Recall the ways you handled interactions with individuals of different races in the past.

- Consider how you might have handled those situations more intelligently.
- To the extent that you handled previous encounters intelligently, pinpoint the keys to your success.
- Use your increased racial intelligence as a tool for being more effective in the future.

Two

THE RACIAL INTELLIGENCE QUOTIENT TEST

I stand by all the misstatements that I've made.
—DAN QUAYLE (FORMER VICE PRESIDENT OF THE UNITED STATES)

INSTRUCTIONS FOR TAKING THE RQ TEST

The purpose of this test is to determine how effectively you negotiate interactions with people of other races. It is not designed to measure racial attitudes or prejudice. When answering the questions, do not select what you perceive to be a morally or socially acceptable answer. Instead, try to put yourself in the place of the main character (indicated by underlining) in each scenario, and choose the one course of action you think makes the most sense in achieving your primary objective.

Chapter Nine contains the scoring key for this test, and an analysis of why some responses are more racially intelligent than others. Originally, we asked respondents to score the test immediately after completing the questions. However, we discovered that many people find it more helpful to score the responses and to analyze them after they've had an opportunity to read the chapters, in which several of the questions are utilized for illustrative purposes.

1. *You are a <u>white supervisor</u> in a corporation that has had complaints of racism in the past. A group of four black secretaries asks to speak to you about their perception of a hostile workplace atmosphere.*

What is your first response?
    a. "I cannot talk to you until I call the company lawyer."
    b. "Tell me what you people want."
    c. "This company has a nondiscrimination policy that we adhere to strictly."
    d. "Tell me what is causing you concern."
    e. "Please put your concerns in writing."

2. *You are a <u>black sales associate</u> in an upscale department store. You sense that white customers often avoid you and gravitate toward the white sales associates. This is a problem for you because the salespeople in this store work on commission.*

How do you handle the situation?
    a. Get angry and tell the white customers that you can take care of them as well as a white salesperson can.
    b. Quit and look for a job in a store with more black customers, because you can never be successful in this environment.
    c. Ask your white coworker to steer some of her customers your way.
    d. Do nothing to alter the situation.
    e. Go out of your way to approach the white customers and help them look past their racial biases.

3. *You are a well-dressed <u>black businessman</u> riding alone in an elevator. The door opens, and a middle-aged white woman enters. The woman moves as far away from you as possible. She is clearly afraid.*

How do you react?
    a. Try to engage the woman in small talk.
    b. Tell her that, even though you're black, she has no reason to be afraid.
    c. Since the woman has already prejudged you as dangerous, move closer to her and flash a sinister smile.
    d. Give the woman a friendly nod, take a step away, and pretend she's not even there.
    e. Suppress your feelings. Do and say nothing.

4. *You are a* <u>white woman</u> *on an elevator that was full of people when you first got on. Suddenly, you notice that everyone has gotten off—except you and a young black man. You feel uncomfortable.*

How do you react?
    a. Suppress your feelings. Do and say nothing.
    b. Start talking about the weather, and hope his friendly response will put your mind at ease.
    c. Put your hand in your purse so he'll think you're carrying a weapon.
    d. Strike up a conversation. Tell him that you're all in favor of affirmative action.
    e. Get off at the next floor and wait for another elevator.

5. *You are a* <u>white parent</u> *taking your sick child to a pediatrician assigned by your new health maintenance organization (HMO). You walk into the examination room to find that the doctor is black. You have no experience with African American doctors, and you're not especially comfortable with the prospect.*

What do you do?
    a. Be pleasant and don't respond to the doctor's color. Allow him to examine your child. Who knows? You may like this doctor.

b. Find some pretense to leave. Walk out of the office. Inform your HMO that you will only accept a white doctor.
c. Congratulate the doctor for getting so far in life. Tell him that he sets a good example for other blacks to follow.
d. Tell the doctor nobody in your immediate family has ever had a black physician before. Admit that you feel a little nervous about his examining your child.
e. Walk out without offering an explanation.

6. *You are a* <u>*white administrator*</u> *who feels uncomfortable because one of your colleagues regularly tells racist jokes when no blacks or Hispanics are around.*

The best way to handle this situation is to:
a. Laugh at the jokes.
b. Immediately tell your supervisor.
c. Do nothing.
d. Contact a lawyer.
e. Take the colleague aside and talk to him.

7. *You are a* <u>*black high school senior*</u> *applying for admission to college.*

Which is your best strategy?
a. Send a letter with the application telling them you are black.
b. List black-identified groups under extracurricular activities or mention them in your essay.
c. Ask to see the school's written affirmative action policy.
d. Make no reference to race.
e. Find out all you can about the school. If you think it will be to your benefit, mention groups and activities that make your racial identification clear.

8. *You are a <u>white supervisor</u> who sees a black employee distributing anti-Semitic material on a street corner after working hours.*

What do you do?
    a. Call the police.
    b. Fire the employee.
    c. Ignore the incident.
    d. Notify human resources.
    e. Confront the employee during working hours.

9. *You are a <u>white professor</u> proctoring a final exam at a college that has had more than its share of racially sensitive issues in recent years. You spot a black student cheating on the test. The rules are clear: Any student caught cheating will be asked to leave the examination hall and given a failing grade on the test.*

How do you handle the situation?
    a. Immediately confront the student. Tell him you saw him cheating, and ask him to leave the room.
    b. Pretend you haven't noticed the cheating, so as not to provoke a confrontation, which could possibly leave you open to charges of racial bias.
    c. Quietly tell the student that if you spot any more irregularities, you will have to ask him to leave.
    d. Call in a black colleague, and ask him to help you deal with the problem.
    e. Let the student complete the test, then call him aside and let him know that you saw him cheating.

10. *You are a <u>white section supervisor</u> who overhears two black secretaries using the "N word" with each other.*

What do you do?
    a. Take no action.

b. Politely tell the secretaries that the "N word" is not to be used on company premises.
c. Tell the secretaries that you are offended by the "N word."
d. Use the "N word" yourself in a humorous fashion.
e. Threaten to report the secretaries to your superior.

11. *You are a* <u>white motorist</u> *driving a late-model car. Suddenly you are stopped on the freeway by a black policeman for going 64 mph in a 55 mph zone. You've been driving this highway for years, and can't ever recall observing the speed limit. However, you always stay within the flow of traffic and have never received a speeding ticket.*

Under the circumstances, how do you react?
a. Point out to the cop that everyone else is going over the speed limit, and ask why he's making such a big deal out of nothing.
b. Ask the officer for his name and badge number. Tell him that this is clearly a case of discrimination.
c. Try to engage the officer in a friendly conversation about black athletes and entertainers.
d. Offer the cop some cash if he'll let you go.
e. Apologize for going too fast, and ask the officer if he'd consider issuing a warning in lieu of a ticket.

12. *You are a* <u>white middle manager</u> *in a large corporation who has been having problems with your computer. Failure to resolve those problems may prevent you from meeting a critical deadline. The person in charge of authorizing computer repairs is a black woman, and you're convinced that she is purposely putting your repeated requests for help on the back burner.*

How do you handle the situation?
a. Confront the woman, and ask why she refuses to help you with your problem.

b. File a written complaint with the woman's supervisor.

c. Let yourself be overheard telling colleagues that the woman doesn't like you because you are a white man.

d. Approach the woman in private. Tell her that you know she is busy, but that you really would appreciate her help. Tell her that if the two of you can't resolve the situation, you will ask others in the department for help in solving your problem.

e. Do and say nothing. Maybe the situation will somehow resolve itself.

13. You are a <u>black employee</u> who has been passed over for a promotion five times. On each of these occasions, you've asked your white supervisor for an explanation, but he has been evasive.

What do you do?
a. File a racial discrimination lawsuit.
b. Meet with your human resources representative.
c. Start looking for another job.
d. Do nothing. Accept the fact that it's hard for blacks to get ahead in Corporate America.
e. Politely confront your supervisor. Insist that he give you specific written feedback about your performance.

14. You are a <u>white employee</u> who enters the cafeteria looking for a place to sit. The only seats left are in the area where a group of black coworkers regularly sit. You feel conspicuous enough about being the only white at the table, but when you sit down, the black diners stop talking and stare at you.

What do you do?
a. Give the employees the "brother handshake."
b. Get up and change your seat.
c. Ignore the other people. Finish eating and leave.

    d.   Confront the other employees about their rude behavior.

    e.   Try to make light conversation with one or two people at the table.

15. *You are a <u>white telemarketing manager</u> who has recently hired a young black man whose job it is to "cold call" prospects for a home repair service. The employee is a superior salesman, but his speech is filled with "black English" expressions.*

How do you handle the situation?

    a.   Say nothing.

    b.   Discreetly present him with a book on standard American English.

    c.   Gently correct his speech.

    d.   Have him practice with language tapes.

    e.   Warn him that he must take speech training or lose his job.

16. *You are a <u>white manager</u> at a fast-food restaurant. You notice that a young white male waiter always seems to have a bad attitude toward the black and Hispanic patrons—though he is a good worker in other respects. You have spoken to him a number of times, but there has been no improvement. Waiters at this restaurant are "at will" employees. They belong to no union and can usually be fired without cause.*

What do you do?

    a.   Fire the waiter.

    b.   Have the waiter serve only white customers.

    c.   Send the waiter to a racial intelligence seminar.

    d.   Call a meeting of the staff and try to get to the bottom of the problem.

    e.   Assign the waiter to dishwashing duty until his attitude improves.

17. *You are a <u>white manager</u> whose company has only a handful of minority employees. One of them is a Muslim, who approaches you and asks to take a day off for the celebration of Eid-El-Fitr, an important day in the celebration of Ramadan. While this is not considered an official holiday by your company, the employee points out that the plant is closed on several Jewish holidays and therefore he should have a right to take off on a day that's important to him.*

What do you do?
  a. Grant the request.
  b. Deny the request.
  c. Tell the employee that he can leave, but he must charge it as a personal day.
  d. Explain that, on the Jewish holidays in question, work is not permitted.
  e. Explain that many more employees are Jewish than Muslim.

18. *You are a <u>black high school senior</u> applying for a bank job. Your guidance counselor tells you to wear a suit and tie for the interview and to take the large earring out of your ear. Your friends say that changing your appearance makes you a sellout.*

How do you handle the situation?
  a. Wear the suit and tie. Tell your friends to get their acts together.
  b. Take out the earring, but dress the way you normally do.
  c. Turn down the interview.
  d. Refuse to sell out. Do what makes you comfortable.
  e. Wear the suit and tie, but tell your friends that you agree with them, so they'll stop bugging you.

19. *You are a <u>white salesclerk</u> in a large electronics store. When a black customer asks if the price of a VCR he is considering is correct, you look at the price tag and say, "Boy! The price on that model must have just gone up."*

There is a pregnant moment of silence. You realize you've acci-
dentally said "boy," an otherwise innocuous term that you fear may
have had an offensive connotation when addressing a black man.

How do you handle the situation so that the customer most likely
will not walk out of the store?

    a. Continue the interaction as if nothing happened. Try to be more careful in the future.

    b. Explain to the customer that you meant "boy" as in "oh boy!" It was not your intention to be offensive.

    c. Talk about how many black friends you have.

    d. Walk away and ask a black salesclerk to attend to this customer.

    e. Try to compensate for your faux pas by engaging the customer in small talk.

20. You are a <u>white cab driver</u> who is new on the job. A few of the
veteran cabbies have warned you to avoid black riders. A young,
neatly dressed black man enters your taxi while you are standing at
a red light.

What do you do?

    a. Ask him where he's going and take him there.

    b. Ask him where he is going. Whatever he tells you, apologize and say that you are about to go off duty and are heading in the opposite direction.

    c. Ask him where he is going. If you don't feel safe in the neighborhood he wants to go to, tell him that you are concerned about your safety. Ask if he'd consider waiting for another cab.

    d. Order him to get out of the cab. If he refuses to leave, call a cop.

    e. Ask him for payment in advance.

THREE

EIGHT STEPS TO MORE EFFECTIVE RACIAL COMMUNICATION

Who said there was ever going to be total understanding? Who said that the only acceptable outcome of any conversation was complete agreement? In a dialogue between a black person and a white one, maybe neither will ever fully understand what the other is trying to say. Maybe it's not about the pursuit of some holy grail of total understanding. Maybe it's about incremental understanding, about gaining ground in spite of friction.

—BRUCE JACOBS (AUTHOR)[1]

Two middle-aged women—one black, the other white—were having a heated argument about their place at a department store checkout counter. The black shopper felt that the white shopper had pushed ahead of her in line, and told her so. The white shopper was adamant about being taken care of first—and went to find the white head cashier, who took the white customer's side. "You'll just have to wait your turn in line," the head cashier told the black shopper—who then went to seek out Harry, the white store manager.

"How did you handle the situation?" we asked Harry.

"I didn't exactly handle it," he answered. "I simply refused to get involved, and walked away."

The black shopper proceeded to abandon her shopping cart and walk out of the store, but not before getting Harry's name and the name of the head cashier.

The next day, she canceled her long-standing account at the store and wrote a letter to the CEO of the department store chain, complaining that she was a victim of racial discrimination. The head cashier was subsequently fired, and Harry received a reprimand and a demotion.

"What, if anything, did you learn from this experience?" we asked Harry.

"One of the things the letter of reprimand said was that the head cashier was wrong in favoring one customer over another, and that my unwillingness to correct her mistake amounted to tacit approval of her actions. I think it's unfair of them to expect me to handle tough situations with no training in this area."

It's true that Harry's employer should have trained employees never to take sides in customer disputes—especially those that have a racial component. At the same time, it was risky for Harry to count on someone else to assume responsibility for making a smart decision.

Harry told us that he viewed the head cashier in this scenario as negatively disposed to African Americans, "someone who would automatically favor the white person in any white-on-black dispute." That cashier is entitled to her feelings, but she is not entitled to act on them. The only thing that matters is what a person does, and that cashier's racially unsavvy behavior got her fired.

According to Harry, his refusal to take sides was driven by an aversion to conflict—not by any inherent racial bias. Here again, Harry's underlying feelings and motivation were beside the point. It was his behavior that trapped him. There are times when you need to disconnect how you feel from what you know to be the smart course of action in any particular situation. This is one of the key skills you will acquire in the process of becoming more racially intelligent. The following eight-step program is designed to help you:

1. Recognize what you have to gain.
2. Don't pretend to be color-blind.

3. Watch, but don't preach.
4. Build on what all of us share.
5. Learn from every experience.
6. Look at it through the other person's eyes.
7. Know what you want to accomplish.
8. Close the deal.

RECOGNIZE WHAT YOU HAVE TO GAIN

Identify the benefits of developing smart strategies for effective racial communication. In today's increasingly diverse work environment, racially smart companies and people are at a distinct advantage over their less-intelligent counterparts.

The more racially smart company has a broader vision of the market, and is less likely to engender complaints, grievances, and litigation. These days, companies are being sued for racial discrimination because of the words and actions of line workers, middle managers, and high-level executives. That's why it's risky to have racially unintelligent employees—no matter what their position or salary.

Corporate leaders have found out how tough it is to shed the label of racism once it becomes ingrained in public perception. That's why companies that are hit with allegations of bias will sometimes go to great lengths to avoid being perceived as another Denny's or Texaco.

A world-famous toy retailer was the subject of a federal discrimination lawsuit, which alleged that a store manager called an African American employee "boy" and told other workers to hide black Barbie dolls. The plaintiffs also claimed that the manager, who resigned after working at the store for less than two months, created a racist atmosphere by saying, among other things, that she would "lighten the complexion of the workforce" and that "there were too many shades of brown in the staff."

The company's CEO responded by accepting the manager's resignation and stating that "the allegations in the lawsuit arise out of the actions of one employee over a two-month period whose conduct we consider offensive and intolerable and completely contrary to [the company's] longstanding commitment to providing equal opportunity to all its employees."

Shortly thereafter, a consultant and an "employee advocate" were hired to conduct diversity and sensitivity training for management. These are the steps companies usually take when they are desperately trying to stave off potential lawsuits and a ton of negative press. However, this particular toy giant apparently went a step further.

After the allegations broke as a lead story on several nightly news programs, the entire incident somehow vaporized. As hard as we tried, we could not find any follow-up in the print or electronic media. While we have no tangible proof, we can only imagine how much money this company spent and how many favors were called in to make the story go away.

Concerns about lawsuits and bad publicity are just part of the reason businesses need to become racially intelligent. Companies that plan to stay competitive understand the question as one of smart economics.

Today's most desirable job candidates are increasingly diverse and sensitive to racial issues. People want to know how minorities are treated at the companies they're considering, and the extent to which different groups are represented in management ranks. Businesses that are perceived to be biased, or as offering little opportunity for minorities to advance, also experience high turnover costs, because talented people want to be judged on merit—not race.

Just as with companies, racially smart men and women have a much better chance of achieving their objectives, and avoiding getting trapped by racial problems.

Employers, managers, and workers of different races who can function in a comfortable and cooperative fashion are going to be more efficient and productive at their jobs. Entrepreneurs and salespeople who know how to deal effectively with customers and suppliers of all races and backgrounds will be more successful in the marketplace.

Without a certain amount of racial smarts, you risk losing a promotion, a sale—even your job. Without the ability to negotiate diversity encounters, you can also create resentment from people who are in a position to make your life miserable.

If, for example, you are perceived to be a racist by a bank teller or a restaurant server, that person can mishandle your transaction— or spit in your soup! If you display your racial ignorance to a cop or a judge, the potential consequences can be even worse.

Racial intelligence requires a certain amount of civility, in terms of treating others as you wish to be treated. Racially smart behavior is always in your self-interest, because it increases your chances of *making the deal*—whatever the deal happens to be.

Making the deal in a diversity encounter can be closing a sale, landing a job, securing a raise or a promotion, or getting a coworker or boss to expedite your project. Making the deal can also be acting in a way that gets you better service at an airline ticket counter or in a hospital. A higher RQ can spell the difference between a judge finding you innocent or guilty, a cop letting you go or writing you a traffic ticket, or a doctor trying just a little bit harder to find the source of your pain.

There are many deals we need to make in the workplace and in everyday life. The smarter you become, the more successful your interactions with people of other racial and ethnic backgrounds will be.

DON'T PRETEND TO BE COLOR-BLIND

Recognize that differences exist between people of different racial groups. These differences are based on their cultures and experiences. Even if you don't understand the exact nature of the dissimilarities, it's important at least to be aware of how they can affect you.

Some of the major contrasts between white and black Americans stem from having a Eurocentric versus an Afrocentric heritage and worldview. But mostly they are a result of the very different experiences people have negotiating the world, based on their skin color.

For example, black people in America report negative interactions with the police four times more often than whites or Asian Americans. This disparity goes a long way in explaining why whites and Asians tend to trust cops more than blacks.

It's important to acknowledge the differences between yourself and others, and to use that awareness to become more effective in your dealings. Noticing differences doesn't mean you're biased. Our research shows that well-meaning people who assume a posture that everyone is—or should be—the same are often ashamed of their true feelings and biases. These individuals may have good intentions. However, when you refuse to accept that real differences exist among groups of people, you increase the risk of inadvertently offending someone.

Daryl, a white junior executive at a dress manufacturing firm, was having a casual lunchtime conversation with some coworkers. One of the men asked Daryl what he thought of a female receptionist's looks.

"It's a Dow Jones situation," Daryl replied—meaning that the woman's looks were up and down, depending on the day. At the time, Daryl happened to be glancing in the direction of a light-skinned black female colleague, who was sitting across from him. She responded to the remark by saying, "For your information, black people know about the stock market too." Then she walked out of the room.

Daryl was miffed by the woman's response. "She has some nerve accusing me of being a racist," he said to the man to whom he'd made the Dow Jones remark. "I don't even think of her as being black."

"You should tell her you were trying to insult women—not black people," the male coworker quipped.

Daryl's friend had a point. Talking about a woman's looks in terms of the fluctuations of the stock market can easily be construed as sexist. But racist? That seemed to him to be a stretch. Daryl still bristles when he thinks about the woman's reaction. "Some black people can't ever get past the fact that they're not white," he told us.

Daryl failed to recognize that his coworker's experience as a black woman is very different from his as a white man. The fact that she has light skin and is often taken for white is irrelevant—at least from Daryl's perspective. If anything, such mistaken identity often makes a person more likely to be exposed to the offhanded racist remarks of people who aren't aware that someone of color is within earshot. Daryl didn't need all this information to handle the situation effectively. He could have avoided getting trapped by his faux pas by simply doing the following:

- Acknowledge that the woman he'd offended had a different set of experiences and sensitivities.
- Refrain from using language that is potentially offensive to any group—be they women or African Americans—especially in the workplace.

Instead of learning from the experience, Daryl is still angry at his coworker, and is at high risk of making other, potentially more serious mistakes.

If you are going to have positive negotiations and achieve your goals, you need to understand that others may be put off by words or actions that are neutral to you. Recognizing the potential impact of differences in culture and experience can help you avoid getting trapped by racial misunderstandings. It's not necessary to be aware of all the specific cultural nuances, and why they affect people the way they do.

WATCH, BUT DON'T PREACH

Try to become a keen observer of racial differences without passing judgment. Understand that these cultural and experiential disparities don't make one person right and another person wrong.

People get attached to their own way of doing things, and to the customs and characteristics of their particular racial, religious, and ethnic groups. For example, some Catholics and Protestants find it hard to accept that not everybody thinks of Christmas and Easter as important religious holidays. Some whites find it hard to acknowledge Martin Luther King Day as worthwhile.

Montaigne, the sixteenth century French writer, made an astute observation when he wrote, "Each man calls barbarism whatever is not his own practice." It's not easy to stop ourselves from judging others from our own frame of reference. After all, our own experience of the world is the only firsthand knowledge any of us has. We sometimes need to remind ourselves that other people's experiences and viewpoints are just as central to their being.

Someone else's beliefs, customs, and opinions may seem strange—or even wrong. But remember, you're making those judgments through the lens of your own culture and limited experience. That's why thinking about racial and ethnic practices in terms of right or wrong is both inaccurate and ineffective.

Once you develop the habit of standing back and simply observing the differences you encounter without passing judgment, people will trust you and talk more openly. You will learn a lot about them, and soon find that you are more effective at negotiating diversity encounters.

BUILD ON WHAT ALL OF US SHARE

People of different races have more similarities than differences. We all want security, peace, and good health for ourselves and our families. Furthermore, we share many of the same moral codes and core values—even if we sometimes express them differently.

For example, Christians, Jews, and Muslims hold many of the same moral values. However, there are some important differences in the way each group goes about expressing them. Blacks and whites also have many shared beliefs. Our research shows that most black Americans have far more in common with white Americans than with black Africans.

There is a lot of talk (especially among politicians) about finding a common ground for bringing the races together. In fact, we don't have to look far for the common ground. It's right there at our feet.

We all feel uplifted when we hear stories of human heroism and kindness. Similarly, we all mourn when we're confronted with news stories of children being gunned down in their classrooms. However, there are other public events that bring our ethnocentric concerns to the fore.

When a British nanny was accused of causing the death of an American baby in her care, there were mass protests in England. It was obvious that some British citizens interpreted the allegations against one of their own as a cultural affront. Not surprisingly, most Americans didn't see it that way. Americans may have been divided as to the nanny's guilt or innocence, but they didn't look at the murder allegations as an outpouring of anti-British sentiment.[2]

The difference in the white and black responses to the O. J. Simpson trial is an example of how public incidents can divide people along racial lines. Many blacks had no trouble believing that Simpson had been framed by racially biased white police. Whites, on the other hand, tended to dismiss race as a factor, and were baffled as to why so many blacks viewed the case in those terms.

Remove race and culture from the equation, and everyone can agree that murder is abhorrent. However, once these factors come into play, they can obliterate more fundamental issues, and cause us to lose sight of the common values that bind us as human beings.

One common characteristic members of all groups share is a tendency to want to be with their own. Yet, this very human trait ends up pushing other groups away. There's nothing sinister in people wishing to associate with others who share a similar background. No one group displays this characteristic in greater measure than any other—though it may appear that way to an outsider looking in.

People demonstrate a lack of racial intelligence when they categorize and stereotype members of other groups. "Those people" may look and sound different from you. They may eat different foods, listen to different kinds of music, and prefer TV personalities who look like them. Still, chances are "those people" are a lot more like you than you might imagine. There's a line in a popular children's song that captures this thought:

We're all the same, but we're different.
We're different, but we're all the same.

Some events and incidents pull people apart. However, racially smart individuals blend this knowledge with an awareness of the many feelings and experiences all of us have in common.

LEARN FROM EVERY EXPERIENCE

Use each diversity encounter as an opportunity to learn about your own mind-set, as well as that of other people. Try to make effective use of this knowledge in future encounters.

We all want to avoid mistakes. Yet, we often learn more from our blunders than from interactions in which things go smoothly. It's impossible to be aware of all the customs, values, and experiences other people carry into each diversity encounter. At some point, your lack of knowledge is bound to result in an uncomfortable situation. Rather than becoming angry or judgmental, it's important to use that encounter as a learning opportunity.

Brian, a third-year medical student of Chinese American heritage, shared with us an experience that illuminates how easy it is to create discomfort when you are unaware of other people's customs and values.

"I was having a conversation with a group of other students between classes," Brian recalled. "At one point, a female classmate who is African American and a practicing Muslim made a hilarious comment about one of the teachers. I laughed out loud and offered my hand for her to 'slip me five.' She just laughed, and ignored my hand.

"'Come on,' I said. 'Don't leave me hanging!' But it was obvious that something wasn't right. I was starting to feel rejected. Was it my breath? Why didn't this attractive woman want to touch me?

"Several days later, I approached the classmate and asked her if she'd mind explaining her reaction to me. She said that it is against her religion to have any physical contact with a male, even to shake hands, unless the person is her husband or a family member. She realized that this was going to be difficult, considering that medicine is a hands-on field. However, she said that she was trying her best to stick with her religion.

"I immediately apologized for making her uncomfortable. I told her that I wasn't aware of this custom, and would be more careful in the future. Since then, I've been sensitive to physical contact with Muslim women."

When you find out something about a person's religious or cultural practices, it's always a good idea to file that away for future reference. Beyond that, it's important to assess your own feelings during the encounter.

Brian acknowledged feeling mildly rejected during the interaction. He didn't suspect that the woman's unwillingness to touch him had anything to do with her own race or religion. Still, as he thought about the incident, Brian felt the need to gather more information. Asking the woman to explain her action was a smart solution. The information he gleaned from this incident may well help him in his personal and professional encounters in the future.

A lack of knowledge in diversity encounters is often less problematic than the stereotypes people bring into situations. It's one thing, for example, to offer an observant Jew or Muslim a ham sandwich, if you're unaware that his religion forbids him to eat pork. It's quite another if, after he declines the sandwich and tells you why, you walk away thinking that he's a rude person whose religious practices are foolish.

When you find yourself making such sweeping negative judgments in response to a diversity encounter, don't deny your feelings. Instead, consider the basis for those feelings, and ask yourself whether you're handling them in the most useful way.

The most constructive way to process nonproductive feelings is to set up a kind of *buffer zone* between your emotional reactions and the potential consequences of how you express them. A computer's buffer zone serves as a shield between what goes in and what goes out. Similarly, a personal buffer zone can give you a chance to separate and process your feelings before you act.

Take the case of a white video store owner who has recently launched a business in a racially mixed neighborhood. The store owner believes that young black customers are more likely to steal tapes than other shoppers. This belief is based on stereotypes, rather than on actual previous experience. Nevertheless, the man has instructed his employees to "stick close to black customers" so that they don't shoplift.

This policy has already created problems for the store owner. Several black customers have complained about being followed. They couldn't help but notice that white customers aren't subjected to this form of harassment. Several community leaders have threatened to organize a boycott of the store if this racially based scrutiny continues.

Put yourself in the store owner's position. You want to avoid a boycott. Still, you can't deny your feelings. In time, the owner may realize that he is operating under a set of false assumptions, and end up changing his policies. But first, he needs to spend some time in his personal buffer zone so that he can find a way to be vigilant while staying out of trouble. The process would go as follows:

- *Acknowledge your feelings.* The store owner in this scenario must first accept the fact that when black customers enter the store, his suspicions are aroused. (No problem so far.)
- *Evaluate the source of your feelings.* The store owner has not had any particularly bad experiences with black customers in his store—or with black people in general. For the most part, his impressions have been formed by news stories about black crime.
- *Find ways to act on your feelings that address your concerns but do not cause trouble.* One possible solution for the store owner would be to install a camera to monitor all the customers. That way, he would be able to pinpoint the actual thieves without harassing legitimate shoppers.

LOOK AT IT THROUGH THE OTHER PERSON'S EYES

Avoid interpreting the thoughts and actions of others based on what they would mean if you were in that position. Recognize that these thoughts and actions usually have a reasonable basis in the person's culture and experience. If you wish, you can try to understand these differing viewpoints, though this is not necessary to raise your RQ.

As long as you can articulate your own point of view, you need only recognize that people of other races have different experiences and different perspectives. You don't have to understand or like those views. But once you learn to stop interpreting what others say and do in the context of your own experience, you will no longer be shocked when these differences arise.

Hank, a thirty-year-old white jazz musician, related the following personal ancedote:

"When I was nineteen, I was in a band with three black musicians. Travis, the drummer, lived in a primarily black urban neighborhood, and we used to rehearse in his basement. Eric, a sixteen-year-old neighbor—who was white and an aspiring musician—usually accompanied me to the rehearsals. He liked the music, and I liked having someone to talk to on the forty-five-minute bus ride to and from rehearsals.

"This went on for a couple of months, until one day Eric couldn't make it to a rehearsal.

"'Where's your friend?' Travis asked.

"'I guess he had something else to do,' I answered.

"At that point, Travis and the piano player both accused me of bringing my white friend along because I didn't want to be 'the only white guy in the house.'

"I felt hurt by that accusation, and started protesting that it wasn't true. After that, things changed. I came for a few more rehearsals, minus my friend. Finally, I stopped coming altogether.

"A few years later, I ran into Travis at a recording session. We both acted happy to see each other, and went out for coffee afterwards. I asked Travis if he remembered the conversation about my friend. He said that he did, and then changed the subject. I haven't seen Travis since that night."

Misunderstandings like this come about when people interpret the actions of others from their own frames of reference, and make no effort to get beyond them. When that happens, relationships can be destroyed.

From Travis's vantage point, Hank's bringing his friend along was a sign that he either feared or distrusted blacks. In essence, Travis was saying, "If I were the only white guy in an otherwise black group, I'd want other white people around to make me feel safe and secure."

Hank still doesn't believe that bringing his white friend along had anything to do with race. From his vantage point, Travis was unfairly accusing him of racism.

"It would have been impossible not to notice that I was the only white guy in the band," he says. "Still, I never felt like I needed other whites around to make me feel secure." On the other hand, Hank recalls feeling a little nervous about the three-block walk from the bus stop to Travis's house, in what he described as an all-black neighborhood. "I did feel a little safer having someone with me," he admits.

With time, Hank has come to a better understanding of how Travis felt. He acknowledges, "If I were in Travis's position, I might have felt the same way. Still, I wish we could have found a way to stop this misunderstanding from destroying our relationship."

You can sometimes recognize another person's point of view by putting yourself in his or her place. But there are other times when the differences in your backgrounds are so great that this is difficult, if not impossible. When you reach an impasse in a diversity encounter, stop and pay careful attention to what the other person is saying or doing. Don't argue or attempt to supcrimpose your frame of reference on the other person's words or actions.

Remember, it's not necessary for you to like—or even understand—another individual's viewpoint to acknowledge that he or she has a right to those feelings. As long as you're honest with yourself and secure in your own views, you'll be prepared to navigate potentially adversarial diversity encounters successfully.

Know What You Want to Accomplish

Define your personal objective in each encounter. Always think before you react. Ask yourself, "What do I want to get out of this interaction?" Once you recognize what matters most in the situation, try to stay with that goal. Don't allow yourself to become side-tracked by superfluous issues, ego trips, or emotions.

"Keep your eye on the ball" is a bromide that applies to more than just sports. The way to achieve your objective in any encounter with another person is to take a careful measure of that individual, then to give that person the kind of input that will move him to do what you want. This is a concept that's often misunderstood by people who haven't grasped how the game is played. Consider the scenario in Question 18 of the Racial Intelligence Test:

You are a <u>black high school senior</u> *applying for a bank job. Your guidance counselor tells you to wear a suit and tie for the interview and to take the large earring out of your ear. Your friends say that changing your appearance makes you a sellout.*

How do you handle the situation?

Young people in their teens and early twenties often talk about feeling conflicted about "selling out." We counter these ambivalent feelings by demonstrating that the real power rests with the person who knows how to control the situation.

"When you're going on a job interview," we tell people like our high school senior, "you have to make the interviewer like you. The way to do that is to give him what he wants—which is a potential employee who'll be cooperative and productive.

"Interviewers usually make a decision about you in a flash, so you have to dress and speak in ways that conform to *their* standards. You can decide not to do that—as long as you're prepared to suffer the consequences. But remember, people aren't going to hire you just because you think you're deserving. They'll hire you only if you get them to like you, and convince them that you can address their goals.

"By giving the interviewer what he wants, you manipulate him to give you what you want—the job. So, in reality, you're not selling out. Rather, it's you who winds up calling the shots."

People lose sight of their goals when they let themselves get sidetracked by thinking about how unfair life can be. For example, black shoppers often complain that they are treated differently from whites—especially in upscale stores. There's plenty of anecdotal evidence and hidden-camera reports to support these complaints of unfair treatment.

In Bloomingdale's, a fashionable department store, a well-dressed black professional and his six-year-old son were intimidated and frisked by security guards who suspected them of shoplifting. The guards claimed they saw him enter the dressing room with three garments, and then come out with only two. Security couldn't find the other piece of clothing, even after the man was strip-searched in front of his son. The guards' suspicions were unfounded, but the incident was traumatic for the man and his young child. The man subsequently filed a lawsuit against the store. As he told a reporter who was investigating allegations of racial profiling at Bloomingdale's and other department stores:

"I tried to go to the right school, get the right job, work for the right company, grow my kids in the right way, live in the right neighborhood, and here's what we face. You feel so violated, so humiliated, so dehumanized . . . like something has been just ripped out of you."[3]

There's never any excuse for dehumanizing or mistreating customers. Beyond that, the practice of being hypervigilant of black store customers is not founded in reality. Studies show that the vast majority of people who commit shoplifting are not black.

Whether this form of racial profiling is de facto corporate policy (a charge no business would ever admit) or the decision of on-site personnel, it is a blatantly unsmart course of action that defeats the primary goal of any moneymaking enterprise. Shoplifting is a major cost factor for retailers. However, stores must balance the benefits of overvigilant security against the costs of defending lawsuits and the negative publicity that can result from a racial incident.

We work with companies to help them recognize and change those potentially self-defeating security policies. Still, such practices are widespread, so where does that leave the black shopper? The answer goes back to the principle of keeping your eye on the ball and taking control of the situation.

Racial profiling is a reality. Aside from being unfair, it's extremely unpleasant to deal with. The question is, how do you negotiate the situation as it exists?

The fact is, black shoppers continue to patronize Bloomingdale's and other stores that have been accused of racial profiling. In general, these shoppers can assume control and avoid trouble, as long as they think, rather than emote. Consider the following scenario:

You're a <u>*young black man*</u> *who enters an expensive jewelry store catering to a rich, white clientele. It's impossible not to notice that the clerks and security guards are monitoring your movements.*

How do you respond? Do you start cursing at them, thus supporting the hypothesis that you really do present a danger? Or do you attempt to elicit a positive response by acting in a way that counters their stereotypes?

The answer depends on your goal. It's one thing if you want to highlight the store's unfair treatment of African Americans. But if you just wish to make a purchase or browse in peace, you need to monitor your emotions and focus on your goal. In that way, you take control of the situation by using positive verbal and body language, and containing your underlying anger at store personnel. If you do that, the suspicions and biases of the people scrutinizing you are likely to get reframed into another hypothesis:

Maybe this guy isn't some poor kid from the ghetto who wants to rob us. Maybe he's a rich stockbroker who's going to buy a $10,000 Rolex watch.

Some might say that this kind of approach is demeaning or phony. Still, that's how smart people play the game.

There's also a flip side to this scenario. People in work situations must be careful not to allow their biases to interfere with their goals. Customer service and security personnel can be fired or sued for harassing customers. At the very least, they can cause customers to take their business elsewhere. That's one reason companies have a large stake in making certain that employees stay goal-oriented.

A white airline ticket clerk may not like Hispanics. However, the workplace is not the forum for venting those feelings. Her job is to make *all* customers feel good about the airline, so they won't fly with the competition.

Remember, the overriding goal of any company or business person is to make a profit, and to increase the customer base. By alienating any segment of the public, you end up defeating that goal.

CLOSE THE DEAL

Generate a response that is most likely to help you achieve your objective in the situation, even if that objective is simply to avoid trouble. This is the end result of a process designed to help you maximize positive racial communication and to avoid getting trapped by racial problems.

Diversity encounters can sometimes provoke powerful feelings. From the point of view of emotional health, it's never a good idea to deny those feelings, and there are any number of appropriate private forums for voicing emotions. However, these forums do not include interpersonal dealings that can have professional or personal consequences.

Jeff, a black psychologist who works with adolescents, told us that it's not uncommon for some of his white patients to refer to their black peers as "niggers." "I always have a visceral response to that term," Jeff told us. "But it would be unprofessional for me to stop my patients from expressing their feelings, even if they're biased. After all, I'm their therapist—not their peer."

You have to exercise intelligence and self-control to achieve your objectives. That means setting up a buffer zone between your emotional reactions and the potential consequences of expressing them, and ultimately allowing your intelligence to rule.

Remember, the main purpose of raising your RQ is to make it easier for you to manipulate diversity encounters in your favor. A higher RQ won't provide you with an outlet for your feelings. What it will do is help you become more effective, so that you can realize your goals and avoid getting trapped.

At first, you may need to walk yourself mentally through all the phases of the eight-step process we've described in this chapter. But with practice, you will be able to focus on this final all-encompassing step: *generating the response that gives you the greatest chance of achieving your objective.*

Every time you have a real-life diversity encounter or you attempt to generate the most effective response to the various scenarios we present in this book, try to go through each of the eight steps in your mind. With a little practice, you'll become more skilled at turning potentially sour diversity encounters into productive negotiations. In time, the process will become seamless and automatic.

Keep in mind that everyone slips up once in a while. When that happens, review the eight-step program, pinpoint the source of your mistake, and use that experience to make you smarter and more effective in the future.

CHAPTER SUMMARY: EIGHT STEPS TO MORE EFFECTIVE RACIAL COMMUNICATION

Step 1: Recognize what you have to gain. Identify the benefits of developing smart strategies for effective racial communication. In today's increasingly diverse work environment, racially smart companies and people are at a distinct advantage over their less-intelligent counterparts.

Step 2: Don't pretend to be color-blind. Recognize that differences exist between people of different racial groups, based on their culture and experiences. Even if you don't understand the exact nature of those differences, it's important at least to be aware of how they can affect you.

Step 3: Watch, but don't preach. Try to become a keen observer of racial differences without passing judgment. Understand that these cultural and experiential differences don't make one person right and another person wrong.

Step 4: Build on what all of us share. Recognize that people of different races have more similarities than differences. We all want security, peace, and good health for ourselves and our families. Furthermore, we share many of the same moral codes and core values—even if we sometimes express them differently.

Step 5: Learn from every experience. Use each diversity encounter as an opportunity to learn about your mind-set, as well as that of other people. Try to make effective use of this knowledge in future encounters.

Step 6: Look at each situation through the other person's eyes. Avoid interpreting the thoughts and actions of others based on what they would mean if you were in that position. Recognize that these thoughts and actions usually have a reasonable basis in the person's culture and experience.

Step 7: Know what you want to accomplish. Define your personal objective in each encounter. Always think before you react. Ask yourself, "What do I want to get out of this interaction?" Once you recognize what matters most in the situation, try to stay with that goal. Don't allow yourself to become sidetracked by superfluous issues, ego trips, or emotions.

Step 8: Close the deal. Generate a response that is most likely to help you achieve your objective in the situation—even if that objective is simply to avoid trouble. This is the end result of a process designed to help you maximize positive interracial communication and to avoid problems.

FOUR

THE LANGUAGE TRAP

Words in the abstract mean nothing. Meaning depends on context. A racial slur . . . can be a sign of bigotry and hate or friendship and intimacy, depending on the context—to whom it is said, by whom, in what tone of voice, and in what circumstances.

—WILLIAM BENNETT TURNER (ATTORNEY, LAW PROFESSOR)[1]

The elimination of racially offensive language isn't necessarily the most important issue in fostering smoother diversity encounters throughout a corporate culture. However, language is often the trigger for a boycott or a lawsuit, especially when it can be proven. That's what happened to Texaco after several top company officials were caught on tape referring to African Americans as "niggers, porch monkeys, orangutans," and "black jellybeans [that] seem to be glued to the bottom of the bag."[2]

That tape surfaced as attorneys for Texaco were defending a multimillion-dollar antidiscrimination lawsuit that had been filed by six African American employees on behalf of 1,400 of their coworkers. The lawsuit charged that Texaco failed to promote minority employees because of their race. Beyond that, there were allegations that black employees were being demeaned. One of the plaintiffs claimed that she'd been called an "uppity . . . smart-mouthed little colored girl" by a white supervisor.

Texaco's lawyers were either denying the allegations or claiming that the company's practices were the product of race-neutral "business necessity." But once the racist quotes on the tape became front-page headlines, it was too late for excuses and rationalizations.

After Texaco's stock plummeted and civil rights leaders organized a nationwide boycott against the company, a settlement was reached: $140 million in damages and back pay for minority employees, another $35 million to set up an independent task force to monitor the company's diversity efforts, and a promise to give minorities better treatment.

As companies like Texaco spend millions of dollars attempting to resolve lawsuits and purge themselves of the stigma of racism, the following questions will continue to haunt their leaders:

- How many consumers will pass up Texaco stations and gas up elsewhere?
- How many gifted nonwhite people will avoid working for a company labeled as "a chamber of horrors for minorities?"
- What are the short- and long-term costs to these companies in terms of image and bad public relations?

One simple step companies can take to avoid these nightmare situations is to encourage all employees to steer clear of biased language—even language that appears to be biased—in the workplace. Individual employees who are concerned about their careers can't afford to rely on employers to help them become proficient at racially smart language. If you're serious about getting what you want and avoiding the race trap, you need to understand the following principles, and to make them part of your operational style:

HOW TO AVOID GETTING TRAPPED BY YOUR WORDS

- Recognize what's behind problem language.
- Never talk to people in your version of "their language."
- Keep your theories about racial genetics to yourself.
- Don't play racial sociologist.
- Don't make it easy for others to misinterpret the meaning of your words.

- Accept that you can't just say what you want—at least not in public.
- Don't abuse your right to say what you want in private.
- When your words offend, look for the right way to apologize.

RECOGNIZE WHAT'S BEHIND PROBLEM LANGUAGE

Based on our research, we've developed three categories of racially problematical language and behavior: *overt*, *covert*, and *accidental*.

<u>Overt racism</u> is characterized by the kind of language that was caught on tape at Texaco. People in such a situation may say they're sorry. Chances are, the only thing they regret is getting trapped by their own words.

It's not our aim to alter people's feelings—even if those feelings are blatantly racist. But when employees feel free to use expressions like "nigger" and "porch monkey" in a workplace setting, it reveals a high level of racial ignorance that hurts everyone else in the company. Our research shows that people who engage in this kind of dialogue tend to have the following five characteristics in common:

- They don't consider themselves racists.
- They grew up in an environment where racially offensive terms were either accepted or regarded as harmless jokes.
- They associate with others who reinforce their biased notions.
- They feel it's their right to say what they want.
- They've had little direct contact with people of different races who are in a position to challenge their views.

People who use overtly racist language in the workplace may not be especially interested in becoming more effective communicators—unless they are in immediate danger of getting sued, or being embarrassed, or losing their jobs. Still, many individuals who harbor racist views are astute enough to recognize the dangers of displaying them in public.

Even overt racists can raise their RQs by simply shutting up! They must face the fact that many of their ideas about race are

abhorrent to others. At best, they have nothing to gain by expressing them. They should refrain completely from using racial epithets
in the workplace or talking in terms of racial stereotypes, and stay
away from coworkers and colleagues who share these views. In this
way, they will minimize the potential for racist dialogue that can
come back to haunt them.

Covert racism occurs when a person's biased feelings leak out—
sometimes despite the person's intentions. Covert racism can take
many forms. For example, a white man might not regard himself as
biased, but he finds himself checking for his wallet after a black
man accidentally bumps into him on a crowded bus. Such reactions
are based on long-held negative associations that can come to the
fore, even if a person consciously rejects any overtly racist feelings.

Covert racism can sometimes be triggered by a public figure's
uninhibited use of biased language. When the white professional
golfer Fuzzy Zoeller joked that he hoped his competitor, the
part–African American Tiger Woods, didn't order fried chicken and
collard greens for an awards dinner, he was roundly criticized and
immediately lost a lucrative endorsement deal; but Zoeller was
undeterred.

Despite getting hit in the wallet, Zoeller repeated the same
remark a few days later, and even referred to Tiger Woods as "that
little boy." When Zoeller next appeared on a golf course, he was
cheered by fans who lined up to have him sign visors, programs,
and admission tickets.

"Cheered for what?" one sports commentator wondered. "He
didn't win anything, he didn't play a spectacular round of golf." Fuzzy
Zoeller was cheered "because he . . . said exactly what so many of
those people seeking his autograph . . . would love to have said."[3]

People who harbor covert racist feelings sometimes find it hard
to contain those feelings. So, when they hear overtly racist language, they can't resist offering encouragement—or joining in.

It's quite possible that one or more of the Texaco executives who
were caught on tape were only covert racists. Like the people who
cheered Fuzzy Zoeller, they were spurred on by the remarks of their
more openly racist colleagues. No matter. When people are caught
using racially biased language in a company that's already under

scrutiny, they will be shown the same door—whether their racism is overt or covert.

How, then, can people recognize and control covert tendencies that result in unproductive language and behavior? The first step is honestly to assess your attitudes and feelings—even if they clash with your conscious values.

This kind of honesty is especially difficult for people who refuse to acknowledge that they harbor feelings that are at odds with their intellectual beliefs. In the course of our research, we became increasingly skeptical when people who were asked to describe how they handled a potentially difficult situation with someone of another racial or ethnic group offered the following kind of answer:

"I don't care if they're black, white, green, or purple. All people are the same. The color of their skin or ethnic background makes absolutely no difference."

One of the first tenets of racial intelligence is to acknowledge differences. All people are not the same. Until you get comfortable with that fact, you're not going to be able to be honest about your own feelings. One white respondent told us that she didn't notice racial differences. Instead, she lived by Martin Luther King's admonition to judge people "by the quality of their character rather than the color of their skin."

This respondent then talked about meeting her future sister-in-law, a young woman from the Philippines. "She seemed to always be frowning and wouldn't look me straight in the eye," she told us. "I took this as a personal insult. Then, a few years later, I visited Manila. I noticed that all the young Filipina women seemed to be frowning and never looked anyone in the eye."

This woman could never admit that her remark was tantamount to saying, "I once met a Jew who was cheap. Later on, I went to Israel and met lots of Jews, and found all of them to be cheap."

People who refuse to acknowledge ethnic and racial differences can't accept that there's a clash between their theories *of* action and their theories *in* action. Consequently, they can use racially offensive language, and never even know it. Such individuals are more easily trapped by racial problems than many overt racists who are skilled at hiding their true feelings.

There has been a lot of political and intellectual rhetoric about getting people to change their attitudes about race. Maybe that's why well-intended individuals sometimes spout platitudes of racial harmony instead of facing up to their true feelings.

Accidental racism. The person who uses inadvertently biased language is often not harboring any particular racist feelings. He or she may unintentionally say something, without realizing that the words are offensive. However, there's often a thin line separating a racist comment from an accidental remark or code word that isn't meant to offend.

People who normally use racially smart language can unwittingly sound like they're using a code word or epithet. If that happens, it's important to minimize the damage, so that you can get on with the business at hand. Think about how you might negotiate the scenario illustrated in Question 19 of the RQ Test:

You are a <u>white salesclerk</u> in a large electronics store. When a black customer asks if the price of a VCR he is considering is correct, you look at the price tag and say, "Boy! The price on that model must have just gone up."

There's a pregnant moment of silence. You realize you've accidentally said "boy," an otherwise innocuous term that you fear may have had an offensive connotation when addressing a black man.

How do you handle the situation so that the customer most likely will not walk out of the store?

    a. Continue the interaction as if nothing happened. Try to be more careful in the future.

    b. Explain to the customer that you meant boy as in "oh boy!" It was not your intention to be offensive.

    c. Talk about how many black friends you have.

    d. Walk away and ask a black salesclerk to help customer.

    e. Try to compensate for your faux pas by engaging the customer in small talk.

Before deciding on the best option, you first have to recognize your mistake, and then take a measure of the situation—and the person's response. As always, it's important to pinpoint your objective. In this case, the goal is to make the sale, so it's especially important to get a sense of how the customer is reacting to your words.

Option *a* may well be the way to go, if you're relatively certain that the customer wasn't offended. If it appears that you're still going to make the sale, there's no reason to draw attention to your faux pas. The customer may not have taken offense at your words, or even noticed them; it can't do you any good to refocus his attention in that direction. Nevertheless, it's a good idea to file this incident away for future reference.

Option *b* can work if the customer indicates that he's been offended by what you said. In that case, it can help to use a bit of self-deprecating humor. For example, you might say, "I've been putting my foot in my mouth all day. Please excuse me." This kind of approach conveys your understanding, without making the situation worse than it is.

Option *c* is the least intelligent choice. Talking about how many black friends you have is tantamount to wearing a T-shirt that says, "I am a covert racist."

Option *d* is an acceptable backup strategy, assuming that there's a black salesclerk close by. Use it if you sense that the customer no longer wants to interact with you, and he's about to walk out of the store.

Option *e* is acceptable, depending on body language and verbal cues your receive from customer.

Now, let's look at this encounter in reverse. You are a <u>white customer</u> who inadvertently says to a black salesman, "Boy, you're sure asking a lot for this VCR." You, the customer, have the power in this situation. Most salespeople aren't going to walk away on the basis of a remark like this. Still, if the salesman appears to be offended, you might want to explain that you meant no offense—simply as a matter of courtesy and civility. However, if all seems well, you are better off simply letting the comment pass—even if you feel bad about possibly hurting the salesman's feelings.

In a one-shot interaction like this, it's often best to keep things simple. Here again, you do want to make a mental note of any slipups, so that they don't happen again when the stakes are higher.

Never Talk to People in Your Version of "Their Language"

People sometimes try to ingratiate themselves to those in different groups by talking in "their language." It's one thing if you're dealing with Latinos, and you have a working knowledge of Spanish that can help foster better communication. It's quite another thing if you try to cozy up to people by doing what amounts to an imitation of their slang and "inside" vocabulary.

You may hear people of the same group talking to each other in a familiar way, but that's not a signal for you to take the same license. The white salesman who tries to cozy up to a black customer by throwing in some expressions he picked up from a black rap artist is going to lose the sale—and he may never know why. In this instance, imitation won't be looked upon as a form of flattery. Instead, the person is likely to take your attempt to be "cool" as a display of the negative stereotypes you are carrying.

Keep Your Theories About Racial Genetics to Yourself

Remember Jimmy "the Greek" Snyder, the late sports commentator and Las Vegas oddsmaker? He was unceremoniously dumped from his job at CBS after he'd casually commented to a reporter, "The black is a better athlete . . . because he has been bred to be that way. This goes all the way back to the Civil War, when the slave owner would breed his big black [man] with his big [black] woman so that he could have a big black kid."[4]

This was a casual conversation over lunch, and Snyder had apparently consumed more than a few cocktails before letting loose with these street genetics. Snyder's remarks were hardly unique, and they probably wouldn't have gotten him fired ten years earlier. But the standard for acceptable language and behavior changes over time—and not just with respect to race.

In the 1950s and 1960s, cigarette smoking was accepted as normal behavior. The idea of a law banning smoking in public places would have been unthinkable in those years. Now you'll be shown the door if you try lighting up in a smoke-free restaurant.

People tend to be nostalgic for the days when they felt free to do or say whatever made them feel comfortable. Jimmy the Greek came out of an era where a casual racist comment was as acceptable in some circles as lighting an after-dinner cigarette in public. But at the time he made his comments, this kind of rhetoric branded a person an overt racist—and potentially tainted any company that employed him.

If CBS hadn't immediately dumped Snyder, questions about the broadcasting giant's racial sensitivity surely would have come to the fore. So, it was "good-bye, Greek."

Jimmy the Greek was haunted until the end of his life, correctly sensing that those ignorant words were all people would remember about him. This was a man who was never accused of being especially sophisticated or discreet. Nevertheless, a higher education—and even a spotless reputation—doesn't mean you can't be branded a racist for speaking in racial generalities.

In 1995, Dr. Francis Lawrence, president of Rutgers University, was discussing post-tenure review at a faculty meeting when he made a casual remark that appeared to link the low test scores of blacks to their "genetic hereditary background."[5] Several weeks later, Lawrence's remarks hit the newspapers, and student groups began demanding his resignation.

Before that incident, Francis Lawrence had been known as a champion of equal opportunity. Suddenly, he was fighting to save his reputation—and his job.

Lawrence called a press conference, admitted that he had misspoken, and explained that what he had intended to say was that "standardized tests should not be used to exclude disadvantaged students on the trumped-up grounds that such tests measure inherent ability, because I believe they do not."

Lawrence handled a tough situation as well as he could, Still, he was lucky to keep his job in an environment of hair-trigger sensitivity to any language that can be perceived as racist.

DON'T PLAY RACIAL SOCIOLOGIST

When the issue of urban crime comes up, people are often really talking about *black* urban crime. Police have sometimes used crime statistics to justify racial profiling—and even outright brutality. So, it's not hard to understand why this is a hot button for many African Americans.

Given the sensitive nature of the topic, you'd expect the scientific director of in-house research at the National Institute of Mental Health to be savvy enough not to bring up studies on monkeys in captivity and aggressive behavior that referred to inner cities as jungles. But that's exactly what Dr. Fred Goodwin did. As a result of the bad publicity generated by this remark, Goodwin was reprimanded and demoted.[6]

If a distinguished scientist can get into so much trouble for making sociological observations that seem to imply racial bias, imagine what can happen to uncredentialed people who engage in this type of discourse.

Al Campanis was general manager of the Los Angeles Dodgers baseball team—a man who had been instrumental in helping Jackie Robinson become the first black baseball player in the major leagues. Campanis was being interviewed by Ted Koppel on *Nightline*. The theme of the show was a commemoration of the fortieth anniversary of Jackie Robinson's breaking baseball's color barrier.

When Koppel asked Campanis why there weren't more black managers and executives in baseball, Campanis answered, "They may not have some of the necessities to be a field manager or a general manager."[7]

Campanis was branded a racist right then and there. He was promptly fired from a position he'd held for decades. His attempts to apologize and explain himself fell on deaf ears—despite the support of several prominent black athletes. The Dodgers didn't want people wondering if Campanis's sentiments were shared behind closed doors by others in the organization, so they cut him loose.

Campanis learned too late that it's a mistake to engage in what amounts to dime-store racial sociology. It's an even bigger mistake to go on national television and spout views that sound very much like the white establishment's tired excuses for racial discrimination.

"People only heard that one thing from me," Al Campanis told a reporter years later. "Then they never wanted to listen to me again."[8]

DON'T MAKE IT EASY FOR OTHERS TO MISINTERPRET THE MEANING OF YOUR WORDS

Ron, a white engineer at a multinational telecommunications company, recalls a passing comment he made to a black colleague that seemed to cool their once friendly relationship.

"It was during a time when American companies were obsessed with the success of Japanese corporations," Ron recalled. "Every few weeks, we had to attend another seminar on doing business 'the Japanese way.' I'd already had more than my fill of the Japanese business model when we received notice of yet another one of those seminars. I happened to see Frank, my black colleague, reading his notice, so I said, 'Hey, Frank, pretty soon they'll be serving sushi in the company cafeteria.'

"Frank just shook his head and said, 'I wouldn't touch that one with a ten-foot pole.' Then he walked away.

"There was a lot of Japan-bashing going on in my company at the time. Still, I didn't think I'd said anything that was racially prejudiced, though Frank apparently took it that way. I should have realized that, as an African American, he might be more sensitive to any remark that even hinted of racism. Frank and I are still cordial but, since that time, I sense a distance on his part."

That incident taught Ron that people don't necessarily take your words the way you hope they will. Keep in mind that comments that may seem humorous or harmless to you can provoke a different reaction from people who don't share your background.

One would expect that David Howard has learned that lesson. Howard was the white District of Columbia official who informed some colleagues that "the new budget would require him to be more niggardly."[9]

The dictionary defines the word "niggardly" as miserly. So it surprised some people (including a number of prominent African American leaders) that the black mayor of Washington accepted Howard's resignation for using a legitimate word that happened to sound like a racial slur. The problem was, some of Howard's colleagues found his choice of words offensive, even if others thought the entire incident was absurd.

"Would you consider me anti-Japanese if I said, 'There's a little *nip* in the air?'" one network news anchor wondered, in the wake of the "niggardly" incident. "Would I automatically be branded anti-Asian if I said that there was a *chink* in the armor of your argument?" another chimed in.

David Howard was eventually rehired. Still, some people continue to wonder why he found it necessary to use such an obscure and easily misunderstood term—especially in a largely African American environment. Was Howard's use of the word "niggardly" an innocent but thoughtless remark? Or was he using the dictionary to cover up his true racist feelings?

Benjamin Franklin didn't cause a stir when he wrote, "By the niggardly treatment of good masters, they have been driven out of the school." In the eighteenth century, there was no *Nightline* and no Internet chat rooms. Besides, anyone who read those words probably knew exactly what Franklin was talking about.[10]

Some might argue that an educated person should still know what the word "niggardly" means, but that's not the point.

In the twenty-first century, it's not bright to drop an obscure term that sounds a lot like a racial slur. "Niggardly" may be a legitimate word. Still, why not say "stingy," or "cheap," or "miserly"—or some other equally descriptive term that's not going to offend people and possibly get you fired?

Remember, the perception of racial bias can be as harmful as the reality. When you use language that even *sounds* like it's biased, you leave yourself open to the speculation of others as to whether what you said was an inadvertent slip of the tongue or a sneaky way of expressing your true racist sentiments.

ACCEPT THAT YOU CAN'T JUST SAY WHAT YOU WANT IN PUBLIC

In general, the use of racially biased language is not a freedom of speech issue, although some have tried to frame it as such. Constitutionally protected speech refers to prohibitions on the government from punishing citizens for what they say. It has nothing to do with speech in a commercial context. Employers have the right to place limits on employees' language and behavior if they interfere with job performance or harm the employer's image. A company can institute dress codes, attendance codes, as well as language and other behavioral codes—as long as they are applied in a nondiscriminatory fashion. If you don't like the rules, you have the right to work elsewhere.

Some people feel they shouldn't be forced to use racially sensitive language. They resent the fact that acceptable words and phrases are always changing.

"Years ago, it was okay to say 'colored,'" fifty-year-old Alex complained. "Then [black people] wanted to be called 'Negroes.' Then 'blacks' and 'Afro Americans.' Why should I have to keep learning a new politically correct vocabulary?"

Alex, a middle manager in a large corporation, expresses the views of more than a few white males—who sometimes also complain that they can no longer call female coworkers "sweetheart" or "honey." The bottom line is that using language that offends coworkers can get you fired, or at least hold you back. But there's also the issue of civility to consider.

What does it cost you to call people what they want to be called? A man named "William" might ask you to call him "Bill." Then, a few months later, he may want to be called "Billy." The following year he may change his mind again, and want you to call him "Willy." And a year after that, he may decide that he prefers "William" after all. Most civil people would just comply with the person's wishes and call him by the name he chooses. So, why should it be any different when it comes to race?

It's understandable that members of minority groups would be especially sensitive about what others call them. Why shouldn't you respect their preferences?

If you find yourself getting angry when people of different racial and ethnic backgrounds ask you to refer to them in a particular way, think about what could be driving those feelings. Are you angry because you believe that your freedom is being taken away from you? If so, keep in mind that your right to say what you want doesn't supersede the right of others not to hear things they find offensive.

The whole point of speaking to others effectively is to communicate your ideas, your requests, and your feelings—and ultimately, to achieve your goals. It makes no sense to use language that offends or that creates a side issue that can prevent you from getting your message across and realizing your objective in the situation.

Mary, a successful real estate broker who works in a racially diverse area, was surprised when a coworker corrected her after she referred to a Chinese family as "Orientals."

"I believe they prefer to be called 'Asians,'" the coworker told Mary in a private moment. Mary had no idea that the preferred terminology had changed years earlier. "I can't count the number of times I've called Asian people 'Orientals' over the past twenty years—sometimes right to their faces. Who knows how many sales and listings that cost me?"

We're not suggesting that you walk around with a book of acceptable and unacceptable terms. However, being racially smart means keeping reasonably abreast of changes in terminology, and remaining open and nondefensive when others correct you.

DON'T ABUSE YOUR RIGHT TO SAY WHAT YOU WANT IN PRIVATE

Following the violent murder in 1998 of a black London teenager by five white boys, there was talk of passing a law that would have made it illegal for people to use racist language in their homes. The proposal to ban expressions of racial hatred behind closed doors was eventually rejected, on the grounds that it would constitute a gross infringement of civil liberties and create a "thought police" culture.[11]

We agree that it's important that people have a legal right to say whatever they want in the privacy of their homes. Nobody can stop you from cracking racial or ethnic jokes—or even making blatantly prejudiced statements. Still, we don't encourage people to use biased language in their homes for two reasons.

• It's hard to compartmentalize your behaviors and actions. People certainly have a right to feel what they want—up to and including racial hatred. However, such sentiments can come out at the wrong time—and cause trouble.

Remember, thoughts and feelings are not behaviors—but language is. Most of us have much more control over what we say than what we feel. The more adept you become at keeping your more biased thoughts and feelings to yourself, the more racial intelligence you're likely to have at your disposal once you step out the door.

• If you have children, it's most important that they develop the skills of effective racial communication early. Today's young people are starting out at a time when expressions of racial bias are not likely to be tolerated. Since kids tend to mimic their parents, it's in their (and your) best interests if you commit yourself to setting a positive, racially smart example. Besides, many young people today are

turned off by overt expressions of racial bias on the part of their parents. (Please see Chapter Ten for a full discussion on raising a racially
smart child.)

WHEN YOUR WORDS OFFEND, LOOK FOR THE RIGHT WAY TO APOLOGIZE

If you make a comment that someone else finds racially offensive, it
rarely does you any good to defend those words—even if the comment is inadvertent.

Consider the experience of Sandra, a white journalist who was
writing a newspaper article about incoming minority freshmen at a
local college. One of the young black women Sandra was interviewing for the piece was talking about her high school experience.

"There was only one white student in the whole school," the
young woman told Sandra.

"Wow, I'd sure hate to be that kid," Sandra said. Suddenly, what
had been a warm and friendly interaction turned ice-cold.

"I was only responding to the anxiety people feel when they're in
the position of being a conspicuous outsider," Sandra told us. "But I
sensed that I'd blown it, and that nothing I could say was going to
set things right. Still, I had to give it a shot.

"I tried explaining to the young woman that I hate situations where
I'm forced to stand out. I was stammering, trying to get the words
out—which must have made me sound totally stupid and insincere.

"The young woman stood up and left, without saying another
word. That was five years ago, and I still feel horrible that she
walked away thinking I was a racist."

When we asked Sandra if there was anything she would do differently given similar circumstances, she said, "Thinking back on how
my remark must have come across, I probably should have offered
an outright apology before trying to explain myself. Something like,
'I can't believe I just said that. Please know that it wasn't my intention to offend you.' Maybe then she would have been more willing
to listen to my explanation.

"Basically, I wish I'd have thought a little longer before blurting out the offending statement. I don't consider myself biased. On the other hand, I hadn't thought about race that much, and never really considered how I might feel if I were black. That experience made me more thoughtful—and a lot more careful in what I say to people of other races."

Remember, no matter how careful and thoughtful you are, there's no way to guarantee that someone won't be offended by your words—or even by the way you apologize.

Consider the experience of Martin, a black college professor who was leading a seminar for a group of social workers.

One of the participants was complaining about the status of black female social workers in the hospital setting. "It sounds like you're at the bottom of the totem pole," Martin observed.

It never occurred to Martin that there was anything racially offensive in his remark. But at the lunch break, a Native American woman who was also participating in the seminar admonished Martin for "using a blatantly anti-Indian slur."

At first, Martin didn't understand the criticism. He soon realized that the term "totem pole" is an American Indian reference. He still couldn't understand why anyone would find it offensive. Nevertheless, he was now being accused of being racially insensitive at best—racially biased, at worst.

What would you do in Martin's position?

   a. Tell the woman that she's wrong. There's nothing offensive about using the expression "bottom of the totem pole." Anyhow, she shouldn't be so touchy.

   b. Enter into a discussion of the literal and symbolic meanings of the expression "totem pole." Inform the woman that this was a relatively minor symbol in only a handful of Native American tribes in the Northwest.

   c. Tell the woman that you're sorry she took offense. But explain that, as far as you're concerned, "totem pole" is a perfectly innocuous term. Tell her that you'll be careful not to use the term when American Indians are around.

    d.   Say, "I'm sorry you were offended. It wasn't my intention to use a disrespectful term."

Option *a* is a nonproductive approach. You are not in a position to tell persons of another race which terms are and are not offensive to them—even if you genuinely believe their complaint is absurd.

Option *b* is probably the least intelligent approach. It sounds like you're taking the intellectual high ground and effectively saying that you know more than she does about her own culture.

Option *c* starts off okay. But again, it's unwise to debate someone of another group about which terms offend them. Also, saying that you won't use the term when American Indians are around amounts to the same thing as saying, "I won't use the 'N word' when African Americans are around."

Option *d* is the smartest response, for a number of reasons. First, it's likely that this statement will put an end to the debate—assuming the person who is complaining doesn't have some other agenda. Also, you're limiting your apology to the statement in question, without necessarily saying that you agree that it is offensive.

Remember, not all apologies are the same. Some apologies are admissions of guilt—which may not be warranted. Others contain qualifiers that render them insincere and useless. Your objective in offering an apology is to assure the other person that you heard the complaint and took it seriously—and that it was not your intention to be offensive. The ultimate goal is to put an end to any debate, and to move forward with the business at hand.

FIVE

SMART WORKPLACE STRATEGIES

[Companies] that show interest in results rather than traditions or procedures . . . will be best for minorities.
   —ROSABETH MOSS KANTOR (HARVARD BUSINESS SCHOOL PROFESSOR)[1]

No organization can provide the psychic nourishment necessary for sustenance and growth. This is something each of us must do for ourselves.
   —CAROLYN CORBIN (AUTHOR, FUTURIST, CORPORATE CONSULTANT)[2]

• Two black employees sue a Pennsylvania furniture rental company because several managers habitually refer to African Americans with expressions like "all of you," "one of them," and "you people." A court rules that these "coded negative terms" violate the civil rights of those employees. A seven-figure out-of-court settlement soon follows.

• Fifteen black workers in a Wonder Bread plant sue the company for $260 million, claiming that managers didn't promote them, told racist jokes, and refused to let them congregate out of fear they might form a gang.[3]

When white managers treat and talk to nonwhite workers in a prejudicial fashion, with whom does the fault lie—the corporate culture or the managers themselves? Consider another related scenario:

• Three current employees and a former employee file a lawsuit against Coca-Cola, alleging the company pays them less and withholds promotions because they are black. The suit seeks class-action status on behalf of at least 1,500 salaried black workers.

The allegations are followed by the kind of response that has become all-too predictable:

"There must be and will be no room for discrimination . . . of any kind against any employee," a senior Coca-Cola executive tells the media. "There will be no tolerance for actions or words which would indicate any other environment."[4]

Nice-sounding phrases, but one has to ask: Who is responsible for promotions and compensation decisions, if not senior management or their designees?

When you plow through all the spin that companies churn out about their commitment to racial and cultural diversity, it's clear that avoiding lawsuits and negative images are the top priorities. The last thing Coca-Cola wants is for its shareholders to get nervous, or for millions of African American Coke drinkers to switch their brand loyalty to Pepsi, or to be a defendant in a multimillion-dollar race discrimination lawsuit. There are, of course, many other good, positive reasons for companies to avoid getting caught in the race trap, including:

• More cooperative and productive work environments conducive to innovation.
• Increased opportunity to take advantage of the largest talent pool.
• Greater potential to broaden the customer base.
• Good public perception that can enhance the bottom line.

Before these considerations can be addressed, however, a company needs to eliminate racially ignorant language and behavior on the part of its employees. Companies that don't take these steps are often run by leaders who are blind or resistant to contemporary racial realities. Not infrequently, these very leaders are the ones who have invested heavily in diversity programs. Unfortunately, throwing money at a problem often isn't the solution—especially when the problem is something as deep-seated as people's feelings about race.

Trying to change the way someone feels is an exercise in futility. Fortunately, people are capable of modifying their behavior without first changing their feelings—if they can see a tangible benefit.

One reason calls by politicians for greater racial tolerance and understanding are usually met with yawning indifference is that people feel they have nothing to gain. That's also why corporate diversity programs frequently have little or no effect on the way people act and speak. The race trap can ensnare senior managers, line workers, or entire organizations. The most vulnerable corporate cultures are those entrenched in antiquated and ineffective ways of doing business.

UNDERSTANDING RESISTANCE TO CHANGE

It is clear that we are living in a world that is increasingly racially diverse, and that changes are needed—both in the way certain aspects of business are conducted and in the way people interact in the workplace. However, as General Electric CEO Jack Welch cautions, this is easier said than done:

"Change has no constituency. People like the status quo. They like the way it was. [That's why] you've got to be prepared for massive resistance."[5]

Holding on to entrenched ways of thinking and acting is part of human nature. Individuals and companies have a hard time letting go of what's familiar—especially when it comes to something as emotionally complex as race. Positive change is often preceded by pain. The question is: How much pain is an organization willing to endure before it starts making changes?

When business leaders don't foster effective racial communication in their companies or continue to deny that problems exist, the resulting fallout can be costly. Fear is one of life's great motivating forces. Which is why nothing puts racial issues at the top of any corporate CEO's priority list faster than a high-visibility discrimination lawsuit, reams of negative news headlines, and the threat of a widespread boycott.

No corporation wants to risk becoming the next Denny's or Texaco—companies that continue to spend untold millions trying to overcome revelations of blatant racism that don't completely fade with time. As hard as they try to remake their image, some of these companies continue to suffer from the public disgrace of having their employees get caught discussing and acting out their racist feelings.

> • There had been numerous allegations of racial discrimination at various Denny's family restaurants. But a critical mass was reached on a cold morning in 1993, when a group of black Secret Service agents waited more than an hour for breakfast in a Denny's in Annapolis, Maryland. Meanwhile, white agents who'd arrived at the same time received prompt service at a nearby table.
>
> The black officers filed a class-action race discrimination lawsuit against the chain, which was combined with over 4,000 other claims, citing a culture of racism silently condoned by corporate headquarters. Denny's employees were accused, among other things, of asking African American diners to show identification before being served, and requesting that they pay before food arrived.[6]

People are entitled to their biases. But it's a mistake to mistreat any customer—much less Secret Service agents who risk their lives in the name of public safety. If your employees do that, you can expect there to be boycotts that will result in an unknown percentage of your potential customers ordering their scrambled eggs and hamburgers at some other restaurant.

Denny's eventually settled the class-action lawsuit for $54 million. The company also signed a $1 billion Fair Share agreement with the NAACP, pledging increased opportunities for minorities in franchising, management, marketing, and purchasing. As we discuss in Chapter Six, however, allegations of discrimination against Denny's have continued to surface.

One aspect of the Denny's story is that the discriminatory behavior was carried out by servers and counter people—low-level employees who generally earn minimum-wage salaries. That's bad enough, but the racist revelations at Texaco that we detailed in Chapter Four served as an even louder wake-up call because they involved upper management.

When four of your senior executives are caught on tape talking about "niggers" and "porch monkeys," mocking a Kwanza celebration, and planning to destroy documents related to a $520 million race discrimination suit, it becomes next to impossible to come up with rhetoric that will convince anyone that your corporate culture doesn't condone racism—at least tacitly.

It's interesting that four months before excerpts from the Texaco tape hit the evening news, an article in *Management Review* had cited the company as a leader in turning racial diversity into a competitive advantage. In that article, a Texaco senior manager gave the following description of the company's policy in dealing with minorities:

"We have a workforce diversity strategy, not a program. A program implies something sitting off in a corner gathering dust; [Texaco's] approach is an organizational change approach. Workplace diversity is part of and tied into company issues and values."[7]

Considering that it was already fending off a multimillion-dollar antidiscrimination lawsuit, the spin Texaco was attempting in the *Management Review* piece was part of an expected strategy that usually goes something like this:

- Continue to ignore or deny charges of racial bias for as long as possible.
- Make some kind of token effort—by hiring a few more dark-skinned people and putting a few superficial programs in place.
- If necessary, reach a quiet out-of-court financial settlement. If you

can't get the plaintiffs to shut up, crank out as much gooey rhetoric as your public relations department can create.

The above strategy isn't just ineffective. It amounts to a conscious effort not to address any underlying problems. Before long, things are likely to get worse. Once people heard what was said on the Texaco tape, it was time for Plan B:

- Place the blame on a few bad apples.
- Label them as cancers on an otherwise healthy corporate culture.
- Punish them if possible.

Texaco proceeded to dismiss one of the caught-on-tape executives, cut off benefits to two more, and suspend another.

We are accustomed to words of repentance and contrition from children who are caught with their hands in the cookie jar, or religious piety from criminals who are about to be sentenced for their crimes. But such sentiments are rarely delivered in so pretty a wrapping as when they are conjured up by a corporate public relations department for a CEO who is worried about stock values.

During the course of this disaster, Texaco's CEO, Peter Bijur, declared his outrage:

"Behavior which violates the company's policies will not be tolerated. Each of us must maintain the highest ethical standards in the way we conduct ourselves."[8]

Shortly thereafter, Bijur declared his company a "beacon of light" to the corporate world:

"[Texaco has] become . . . a symbol of the broader issue of workplace fairness and equal opportunity in America today. The moment is now and the responsibility is ours to demonstrate to the nation that discrimination can be eradicated. We will work ceaselessly and tirelessly, day after day, to build a company of undisputed opportunity for all individuals."[9]

It would have seemed far too cynical for a CEO facing a national boycott and a discrimination lawsuit to say something like, "How could four of my senior people have been stupid enough to get caught using that kind of racist language—especially after we've invested so much money in diversity training? That kind of dumb language and behavior has to go! Meanwhile, we're going to spend as much as necessary to convince people that we are a haven of racial diversity and sensitivity."

Three short years after the tape became front-page news, *Fortune* magazine ran an article detailing some impressive statistics to back up Texaco's evolution "from pariah to paragon wannabe." And Texaco's Bijur was out there, counseling other companies on how to avoid similar pitfalls.

Despite this apparent turnaround, people continue to wonder "if what's going on at Texaco represents essential, fundamental change, or merely cosmetic alterations," according to the article. After he cited Texaco's progress, the author of the *Fortune* piece noted that the company is "still perceived by many as a chamber of horrors for minorities."[10]

Regardless of whether Texaco succeeds in changing public perception, think of how much money and time this company has spent addressing problems that stem from a refusal to embrace change. Consider how much better off organizations are when they can use resources for innovation instead of covering up for racial stupidity. We recommend the following strategies for any company that wants to avoid getting trapped by racial problems.

Ten Racially Smart Strategies for Organizations

1. Test all present and prospective employees for racial intelligence. Many companies already give tests for personality characteristics, such as honesty, before hiring a new worker. An individual's RQ is no less important.

2. Make certain that team members at all levels understand that they are responsible for behaving and speaking in a racially smart fashion.

3. Institute programs that promote a more merit-based workplace.

4. Get rid of ineffective diversity programs, or those that exist only for show.

5. Constantly monitor criteria for hiring and advancing employees to ensure that discrimination isn't influencing these decisions.

6. Make sure that all employees recognize the tangible benefits of adopting a smart approach to diversity encounters in the workplace.

7. Make it clear that racially biased language and behavior will not be tolerated.

8. Don't attempt to discourage employees from affiliating with members of their own group.

9. Give all employees ample opportunity to have a variety of experiences and contacts with members of other racial groups.

10. Forget about trying to get people to change their feelings. Focus only on developing racially smart behavior.

UNDERSTANDING HOW MANAGERS AND WORKERS CAN AVOID RACE TRAPS

Before a company is forced to pay money to resolve a race discrimination case, its leaders will often try to push the blame downstream, to lower-level managers or even line workers. Which brings to mind a key moment in John Steinbeck's classic novel *The Grapes of Wrath*.

A rifle-wielding sharecropper whose farm is being repossessed by a bank threatens to shoot the employee whose job it is to issue the eviction papers. The ensuing dialogue goes something like this:

Bank employee: "It's not my fault you're getting thrown off your farm. It's the bank."

Farmer: "Who is this bank? I'd like to shoot him."[11]

It soon becomes clear to the farmer that there is no person he can shoot. When it comes to race discrimination lawsuits, however, the aggrieved person(s) can take aim at both the conveyer of racism and the company he works for.

Several recent judgments have ruled that managers and supervisors can be held liable for discriminatory behavior. However, under the legal principle of *respondeat superior,* a company bears the primary responsibility for the actions of its employees while they're on the job.

If a worker runs someone over in a company truck, for example, the company is liable. Likewise, if a manager or line worker engages in racially discriminatory behavior, the company can fire that employee. But ultimately the company must assume the costs of settling the case.

This legal responsibility ought to be reason enough for companies to help every employee become racially smarter. At the same time, it's risky for individuals to count on their employers to assume all the responsibility and get them off the hook.

Consider what happened to Jack, a fifty-eight-year-old former senior manager at a midsized manufacturing corporation. Over the course of Jack's tenure, a growing number of black and Latino employees had filed complaints, stating that they were not achieving the same level of advancement as comparable white employees. These complaints were brought to Jack's attention by managers— all white males who were several rungs below him in the company hierarchy.

"When I asked these managers about those reports," Jack recalled, "I was told that they had no basis in fact. I don't remember any overt racist language in these discussions. But thinking back on it, there was an undercurrent of discrimination in the way these managers brushed off the complaints as 'sour grapes' by troublemakers who'd been passed over for promotion. It didn't take much to convince me that these grievances were not race-related. I thought I had more pressing business, so I left it to the people under me to handle the discrimination complaints."

The situation continued to fester, until several minority employees filed a civil rights complaint with the Equal Employment Opportunity Commission—the agency that enforces federal laws prohibiting unlawful discrimination in the American workplace. A $7 million settlement followed.

The company's board of directors held Jack directly responsible, and he was subsequently dismissed. Jack was outraged by this blow to his career. He continued to believe that there was nothing valid in the discrimination complaints, and that he was a convenient scape-goat for policies that were out of his control. When Jack studied the situation in more detail, however, he found that there was a pattern of discrimination in the way the company advanced minority employees.

"I should have been more aware of what was going on," he says now. "Instead, I took my subordinates at their word, and assumed their recommendations weren't racially based. I also had to face the fact that my lack of due diligence may have stemmed from my personal discomfort in confronting racial issues."

Jack eventually found a management position at another company, though at a significantly lower level than the one he'd previously held.

When we asked him what he would do now if he was faced with similar circumstances, Jack said, "When I'm confronted with any issue that has to do with diversity, I make it my business to look into the matter myself. Then, I deal with every one of these situations as if it's my sole responsibility. I've learned the hard way that you can't delegate this kind of responsibility to those under you, and that you'd better not count on your bosses to back you up when trouble strikes."

PROACTIVE STEPS FOR EFFECTIVE WORKPLACE COMMUNICATION

Any person or organization that is truly interested in avoiding the race trap needs to become proactive—that is, to take action before trouble strikes. There's a fine line between manageable turbulence and real trouble. By the time most people cross that critical line, they've already been demoted, fired, or hit with a lawsuit. At that point, it's too late for preventive measures.

To use a medical analogy, crossing the line is the difference between dealing with high cholesterol or a heart attack. Both circumstances are treatable, but one requires far more drastic measures than the other. No matter what the state of the corporate culture in which you work, you can be effective in your diversity encounters and you can avoid racial problems by adapting the following proactive steps:

Cultivate a Smart Operational Style—Not a List of Rules

Every program or plan for change needs to start off with guidelines. The steps for increasing racial intelligence are detailed in Chapter Three. Like behaviors that enhance physical health, racial intelligence is best achieved when it's approached as an operational style, rather than as a list of rules. Research shows, for example, that restrictive diets aren't nearly as effective as a healthy lifestyle that incorporates a sensible combination of moderate exercise and balanced eating.

So it is with becoming racially smarter. Specific rules have their place, in terms of prohibiting biased language or setting specific criteria for promoting people on the basis of merit and superior performance. However, a laundry list of dos and don'ts won't accomplish nearly as much as a racially smart operational style that transcends rote responses to specific situations.

For example, you can tell people that members of group X find direct eye contact to be rude and confrontational, rather than a sign of forthrightness. Therefore, when you're dealing with someone from group X, don't look him in the eye.

Keep in mind, however, that there are literally hundreds of culturally based gestures and words that can have unexpected connotations to people who are not familiar with them. There are also many exceptions and wide variations within every group. Attempting to memorize lists of cultural rules is a waste of time. People who are effective in handling diversity encounters are aware that racial and cultural differences exist, and understand that it's always counterproductive to be judgmental.

Adopting the more global precepts of racial intelligence into a fluid style comes with experience and practice. Still, you can start reaping the benefits of a higher RQ in your next diversity encounter.

Assume, for example, that you are interacting with someone of a different race, and that person won't look you directly in the eye. Instead of judging the individual as rude or evasive, consider the likelihood that the unfamiliar behavior has a logical basis in that person's background and experience—even if you don't understand it and it makes you uncomfortable.

Disconnect Feelings from Actions

Psychotherapists often instruct patients to get in touch with their feelings. That's also an important concept in negotiating with others. Like gender, socioeconomic status, and education, race and ethnicity generate feelings that significantly influence behavior. Race can impact behavior, even when you're interacting with people of the same background, but its effect is especially profound in diversity encounters.

As you evaluate the way you negotiate interactions, it's important to assess your feelings about race, not for the purpose of changing them, but for making certain that those feelings don't impede your effectiveness. For example, unrecognized attitudes of racial bias can cause you unconsciously to favor a person of your own race over somebody else who is more qualified.

It's natural to feel most comfortable with your "own kind of people," and somewhat threatened by those who are unfamiliar. You may also have a hard time picturing people of different racial groups succeeding in certain positions. These feelings are not at all unusual, but it's risky to allow such emotions to govern your actions and decisions in a business context.

Jim, a personnel manager at the New England–based home office of a major retailer, was asked to hire someone to redesign the company's computer systems. A number of people interviewed for the position. On paper, the best qualified person was an African American woman with a thick Southern accent.

"Despite the evidence, I just couldn't envision this person as a computer whiz. I was more favorably disposed to a nerdy white guy or a young Japanese fellow who were also applying for the position.

These two men impressed me as being more suitable for the job, even though their qualifications and track records were not as impressive as the woman's.

"There had been an ongoing push for diversity in my company, so I hired the Japanese man. I figured if I wasn't hiring a black, I'd better at least hire an Asian. He turned out to be reasonably competent—nothing great. However, the African American woman wound up becoming an innovator in her field. She has since won numerous awards for her outstanding contributions.

"I never got called on the carpet for allowing such a talented person to get away. But I had to face the fact that I allowed myself to be swayed by stereotypes rather than facts that were right in front of me."

Jim found out that hiring and promoting on the basis of race is not smart business. Even though he didn't get fired or demoted for his wrong-headed personnel decision, Jim knew that he cost his company a valuable contributor. Organizations that hire and promote employees on the basis of merit and results will have a competitive advantage over those that insist on sticking to traditions and stereotypes that no longer make sense.

It's important to identify such potentially damaging feelings, and disconnect them from your actions. Without this kind of buffer zone between how you feel and what you do, there's bound to be trouble. In addition, it's essential to make certain that the people you supervise do the same.

Larry, a senior manager at an international telecommunications giant, talked about an experience he had in this regard. Larry had recently begun to do business in China, and wanted a secretary who could speak one or two Chinese dialects in addition to English.

Larry's previous secretary had recently been promoted to his executive assistant, and he asked her for input in the hiring decision. A temporary worker was found to fill in, while Larry and his assistant continued to interview other prospects.

At one point, an Asian American secretary who spoke Mandarin applied for the job. Larry was pleased with her qualifications—including her fluency in the language. However, his executive assistant convinced Larry to hire the temp, even though she spoke no Chinese.

Larry deferred to the assistant, largely because she would have closer day-to-day contact with the secretary than he would. A few weeks later, Larry found out that the newly hired secretary was born in Ireland—as was the executive assistant. Larry suspected that this played "too great a role" in the hiring decision. "I was committed to bringing the best person for the position on board," he recalled. "It blew my mind that my assistant put her personal comfort ahead of my needs and, ultimately, those of the company."

Keep in mind that the best person for the job may be someone racially different from you—and from most other people in the company. Who knows what race will produce the next great artistic or scientific genius? Nobody can predict the color or ethnicity of the person who will discover a cure for cancer. What we do know, however, is that it's smart business to hire and advance the best and brightest people. This is not affirmative action—just good business sense.

If you don't seize the chance to hire the most capable people, someone else will. If you do hire such people, and then fail to reward them based on their accomplishments, they will eventually go elsewhere.

Think about it: Why would a talented person of any color accept a position at a company that spouts a lot of tired rhetoric about equality and diversity, when he or she can choose a company where people are judged on the basis of merit?

Understand Your Capacity for Risk

Like it or not, race remains an explosive and divisive force in our culture. One consequence of this reality is that good intentions aren't always enough to keep people from getting trapped. You also need to use sound racial judgment.

Consider the story of Ruth Sherman, a white, twenty-seven-year-old, first-year elementary schoolteacher in Brooklyn, New York. Sherman assigned a book entitled *Nappy Hair* to her mostly black third-grade class. This award-winning work by an African American author centers around a girl's discovery of self-esteem and racial pride. Though widely praised by reviewers and educators, *Nappy Hair* was not included in the school system's required reading list.

A mother of one of Sherman's students found some photocopied pages from the book, and noticed that they contained some black slang and illustrations of a black girl with wild, "nappy" hair. She immediately became outraged over what she perceived to be a clear-cut case of racism. This mother made copies of the pages and distributed them to other parents—none of whom were familiar with the book or cared about its intent. A group of hostile parents emerged, including several who physically threatened Ruth Sherman at a school meeting.

"You better watch out!" one shouted.

"We're going to get you!" another warned.

School officials tend to act a lot like corporate leaders when trouble strikes. Too often, they are far more interested in appearances than in doing the right thing. The response of the district superintendent to the plight of this terrified young teacher was to give in to community pressures. The superintendent pulled her out of the classroom and reassigned her to desk work. Meanwhile, school officials tried to determine whether Ms. Sherman was "racially insensitive."

Even these bureaucrats could not find fault with the actions of this young teacher. But this provided little consolation to Ruth Sherman—who was both frightened of the hostile parents and disappointed in her superiors for their lack of support.

By this time, the *Nappy Hair* story had become headline news, and public opinion was clearly in the teacher's favor. Rudy Crew, New York's schools chancellor, who at first refused to back Sherman, sent her a hand-delivered letter, complimenting her "dedication and concern for the children." But the gesture was too little, too late.

Sherman experienced nightmares and stomach problems in the wake of the threats, and decided to transfer to another school district. Still she was unable to leave her problems behind.

"I'm not happy about [her coming here]," said one mother at the new school. "I think what she tried to teach was racist and offensive."

"I am very concerned about her being at my daughter's school," added a father.[12]

This is one of the most problematic race-related public incidents we've come across. On one hand, we don't believe that people ought to let the ignorance of others affect the way they make decisions. On the other hand, it's important to be aware that even well-meaning actions can sometimes lead to trouble.

There are times that circumstances compel a person to take a stand, like a manager who resists pressure to give an untrue evaluation to a substandard employee. Such situations are different from those in which an individual chooses to make a controversial statement or introduce material that can be perceived as racist. Here, that person should do everything possible to anticipate the consequences.

Put yourself in Ruth Sherman's place. How good are you at dealing with other people's racial anger? Some people handle controversy and hostility better than others. It's important to gauge your own threshold, and act accordingly.

It's possible that parents would have jumped on *Nappy Hair* even if a black teacher had assigned it. Still, it's unlikely that the repercussions would have been as severe as those suffered by a white teacher.

That may strike some people as unfair. Then again, it's not uncommon for African Americans to use the "N word" with each other, just as Jewish comedians can get away with self-deprecating ethnic jokes. This kind of "inside" language or humor doesn't necessarily appeal to everyone within a particular racial or ethnic group. However, it would be intolerable coming from someone outside the group.

Teacher Ruth Sherman had nothing but high-minded intentions in presenting *Nappy Hair* to her students. Still, the question remains: Was it smart of her to introduce language and concepts that could be perceived as racially charged? It probably would have been a good idea for her to get support from the school administration before she started using the book.

Ruth Sherman's story is poignant because she appears to have been a racial innocent who never imagined that she could get trapped by her own good intentions.

Don't Abandon Your Principles for Fear of the PC Police

Discrimination lawsuits have become so common that there is now a burgeoning market for insurance policies that insulate companies against such legal action. To obtain this coverage insurance companies recommend that senior management take the following steps:[13]

- Make it understood that all employees are employees "at will"— and can be terminated with or without advance notice, so long as no laws are violated.
- Distribute and post all required information and policies regarding discrimination and harassment—as well as procedures for filing complaints.
- Publish and distribute an employee handbook, detailing company policies and procedures in all areas of employment, including job descriptions and expectations.
- Require periodic written reviews of all employees.

These are good procedural steps in terms of meeting an insurance company's requirements. However, they don't begin to address the underlying problems.

For example, written statements of policy and procedures can be distributed throughout a company. However, there is no guarantee that people will follow them. Virtually all companies—including those that discriminate—can showcase official written guidelines that forbid those behaviors. Such policies often exist for appearance, and do nothing to address real issues.

On the other hand, a nonwhite person may deserve to be fired or denied a promotion, and still claim to be a victim of discrimination.

Does this mean that white managers should turn a blind eye to evidence of poor performance, just because an employee is a minority?

Such situations can be delicate, to say the least. However, on balance, it's usually unwise to compromise your principles simply to avoid trouble or create the appearance of racial sensitivity. Still, you do need to step carefully when venturing into such tenuous terrain.

Ralph is a white executive with a large advertising firm. In recent years, his company has required him to attend numerous courses and seminars in diversity and racial sensitivity. "Our CEO is very sensitive to diversity issues," Ralph told us. "In spite of that, many of the people here are clueless in their dealings with people of other races."

Several years ago, Ralph was asked to supervise three young account executives who were slated for "fast track" status. Two were white males; the other was a black female. Ralph described one of the white males as "superior in his performance," and the other white male as "okay." He rated the black female's performance as "below par—even for someone who wasn't on the fast track."

Ralph immediately recognized that he'd been thrust into a delicate situation. There was a widespread feeling among many of his colleagues that minorities were sometimes given special consideration. This contention was vigorously denied by the CEO and other corporate leaders. However, as Ralph noted, "It's almost impossible to get someone in a power position to admit to any sort of preferential or discriminatory behavior."

Ralph was uncertain about how to handle the situation. It crossed his mind that higher-ups may have been pressured into putting the African American woman on the fast track, and then leaving it to Ralph to give the woman a poor evaluation. If the woman claimed there was discrimination, the blame would fall on him.

At the same time, Ralph felt that he had built his success in the company through superior performance and principled dealings with colleagues and subordinates.

"I decided that I was not going to bend the rules for this person—just because she was African American and a woman," Ralph told us. "Which is not to say that I wasn't going to provide all the help and support she required. I went out of my way to be supportive, but I treated the two other new people the same way. I monitored the progress of all three very carefully, and documented all my observations and evaluations.

"The woman's performance never improved during the time she worked with me. I was supposed to formally evaluate her after ninety days, but she was transferred to another department after two months. However, I was required to submit a written assessment of her performance—which I did.

"This person and I had a positive interaction, and she didn't seem to blame me for her transfer. She is still with the company, in another department—but not on the fast track."

Ralph handled a potentially tricky situation effectively. In cases like this, it serves no positive purpose to sacrifice veracity to appear politically correct. When the time comes to fire an unproductive employee, it is extremely difficult for a supervisor to explain away a stack of false, but glowing past performance reviews.

A similar dilemma to the one Ralph encountered was presented in Question 9 of the RQ Test:

You are a white professor proctoring a final exam at a college that has had more than its share of racially sensitive issues in recent years. You spot a black student cheating on the test. The rules are clear: Any student caught cheating will be asked to leave the examination hall and given a failing grade on the test.

How do you handle the situation?
   a. Immediately confront the student. Tell him you saw him cheating, and ask him to leave the room.
   b. Pretend you haven't noticed the cheating, so as not to provoke a confrontation, which could possibly leave you open to charges of racial bias.
   c. Quietly tell the student that if you spot any more irregularities, you will have to ask him to leave.
   d. Call in a black colleague, and ask him to help you deal with the problem.

e. Let the student complete the test, then call him aside and let him know that you saw him cheating.

The white professor in this scenario would probably select option *a* if the cheating student were white. However, she might hesitate to take that course with a black student, for fear of being accused of racial discrimination or profiling.

People of any color who are caught cheating are likely to say anything to avoid being punished. (In that respect, they closely resemble corporate CEOs trying to squirm their way out of legitimate charges of discrimination.) In any case, choice *a* is the only principled—and racially smart—option for the white professor.

It's one thing for the professor to observe the cheating student's race, and to ponder the consequences of administering the appropriate punishment. But ultimately, a person facing a decision in such a scenario will almost always be better served by choosing the truth over fear of being called a racist.

All individuals and companies must strike a workable balance between veracity and politics. That sometimes means making difficult decisions that strengthen—rather than corrupt—yourself, the people around you, and your organization.

TEN SMART GUIDELINES FOR INDIVIDUALS

1. Recognize your own emotions and their potential effects in diversity encounters. Don't allow potentially destructive feelings to govern what you say and do.

2. Take responsibility for your own racially smart behavior, and encourage the people you work with to do the same.

3. Don't rely on your company to implement sensible policies, or expect people above you to take the heat when problems arise.

4. Cooperate with others in your organization—whatever their racial or ethnic background.

5. Concentrate on your own objectives. Don't get sidetracked by office politics or other people's negative agendas.

6. Avoid coworkers who are biased or racially dumb. People like this are often looking for allies, or at least an audience for their biased remarks. If the racially stupid person is someone you like, remind him that people have the right to say and do what they want in their homes. However, that right does not extend to the workplace.

7. Use diversity encounters to leverage your own interests. Instead of viewing people from other racial groups as a potential threat, use the differences between you to develop new problem-solving approaches and to generate new opportunities.

8. Embrace change. Comfort zones have their place, but they can sometimes impede or prevent you from achieving your objectives. Your success in business hinges largely on your ability to harness change into a positive force.

9. Know your tolerance for confrontation. Racial intelligence is an applied set of skills. Different people use it in different ways. For example, if you find yourself in a discriminatory work environment, only you can decide if your best course is to go elsewhere or to pursue a formal complaint.

10. Don't hesitate to use race to your advantage. If you have an opportunity to advance, always take advantage of it. If your race enhances that opportunity, so much the better. There are so many times that race is a detriment, it makes sense to use it when it works for you. If others feel that you were advanced at their expense, don't let that become your problem. The best way to counter such criticism is by doing a great job.

SIX

SALES AND CUSTOMER SERVICE

What people want is to be recognized . . . treated relevantly, and respected for their culture and the heritage that their culture represents to them.
—AMY HILLIARD-JONES (MULTICULTURAL MARKETING CONSULTANT)[1]

People tend to think of selling as a simple matter of talking a person into buying or doing something. But when you get right down to it, selling is an important part of every business and professional interaction. That's true if you're a manager trying to motivate employees, an entrepreneur trying to build a client base, or a job seeker trying to impress an interviewer. The ultimate goal of all business encounters is to generate a positive response—that is, a *yes*. To do that, you have to sell.

Once you look at selling from this broader perspective, it becomes clear that the specific product, service, or idea you're ultimately trying to sell is only one aspect of a complex exchange, in which you as a communicator must take into account a number of mediating factors about yourself and your customer. Race and ethnicity are especially important considerations in diversity encounters.

The following ten racially smart sales principles will help you negotiate this terrain effectively:

1. Treat everybody like a valued customer.
2. Build effective racial communication into your customer service policies.
3. Serve the broadest customer base.
4. Don't let your biases—or those of your customers—stand in the way of a sale.
5. When in Rome, don't start rapping.
6. Avoid using code words.
7. If you don't have anything productive to say, shut up!
8. Make your customers feel good—about you and themselves.
9. Sharpen your listening and observation skills.
10. Negotiate to a close.

TREAT EVERYBODY LIKE A VALUED CUSTOMER

Traditional salespeople see customers as end-users of their products or services. However, smart businesspeople understand that the concept is a lot more inclusive than that. The most useful attitude is to view anyone you come in contact with in the course of doing business as a customer—whether or not that person is in a position to address your immediate goals.

There are different categories of customers, but all of them respond positively to sensitive and considerate treatment. Some serve your short-term needs; others enhance your long-term career objectives. There are external customers, the end-users of products and services, who are the traditional targets of a sales or advertising campaign. There are also internal customers, a category that includes all the employees within a company, as well as the vendors and suppliers with whom the company does business.

In the broadest sense, customers also include competitors and individuals who are trying to sell you something, since they may be in a position to help you in the future. People you meet in nonbusiness contexts can also wind up as direct customers or contacts who can refer customers.

The first rule of taking an effective customer service approach is to treat people the way you would like to be treated in a similar situation. No matter how good the product or service you provide—or how impressive your level of technical talents—so-called people skills can be at least as important to your ultimate success as the item that you're selling.

We often have to remind our medical students and resident physicians that their patients are customers, not just numbers on a chart. Unfortunately, medical schools—as well as law schools and M.B.A. programs—don't spend much time training students how to use good manners and common sense. At this writing, no school we know of offers a course that addresses the principles of smart racial communication—though we are working to change that.

Our research shows that highly trained professionals must possess racial intelligence and other interpersonal skills in order to achieve their full career potential. That's true of anybody who needs to transact business with other human beings.

There was recently a TV ad that went something like this: "We didn't learn the rules of business in graduate school; we learned them in preschool."

The rules of smart business often have less to do with sophisticated concepts than with the values you learn growing up. Things like, "Treat others the way you'd like to be treated," "What goes around comes around," and "You'll get further with a smile than a frown." Our approach to racially smart customer service embraces these homespun values.

Today, the emphasis seems to be more on expedience and technology than on personal service. Which is exactly why individuals and companies that demonstrate intelligence and sensitivity in dealing with customers are at a greater advantage now than at any time in the past.

As increasing emphasis is placed on computers and other impersonal ways of exchanging information, people with racial intelligence and other "high-touch" communication skills will have a clearcut edge over their competitors, because they are offering added value to their customers.

When you give customers more than they expect, your efforts will be repaid. Nobody ever loses money by treating people with respect and consideration.

Some department stores will exchange or refund money for an item under virtually any circumstance—even without a receipt. Sure, there are people who will take unfair advantage of such a customer-friendly policy. But the business leaders who set these guidelines aren't naive—they're smart. When customers feel well-treated, they spread the word, and that translates into more business and less time dealing with problems.

BUILD EFFECTIVE RACIAL COMMUNICATION INTO YOUR CUSTOMER SERVICE POLICIES

It's essential that customer-friendly policies be applied in a nondiscriminatory fashion—which is not to say that racial differences should ever be ignored. People know when they're being well-treated, regardless of whether racial and cultural differences factor into the equation.

In a sense, race is like a catalyst—something that remains the same but has the potential to alter events and outcomes. When people feel they've been treated shabbily in the course of a diversity encounter, race can quickly become a negative factor. And if a company or individual has demonstrated a pattern of racial bias in the past, it becomes increasingly difficult to avoid getting trapped.

In Chapter Five, we talked about the allegations of racism at Denny's restaurants, as well as the ensuing class-action lawsuit and $54 million settlement, after Secret Service agents claimed that servers did not give prompt service.

In the wake of that 1994 lawsuit, the executives at Denny's and its corporate parent, Advantica Restaurant Group, suddenly realized that its reasonably priced family restaurant chain would not be able to survive without black and Hispanic customers. Since then, corporate leaders have been working overtime to shed Denny's racist image.

"As this country grows in the next fifteen years, [its] racial composition ... will change dramatically," said John Romandetti, Denny's chief executive. "And if you're not in touch with the tastes of minorities or in a position to reach them through ads, you're going to miss an incredible opportunity."[2]

We would add that, if employees continue slighting and insulting nonwhite people when they come into an establishment, it's going to be tough to convince the public that discrimination is a thing of the past.

Denny's chief diversity officer has admitted, "There were no clear-cut policies against discrimination, and there was no racial sensitivity training. Now, [Denny's policy] is very specific: If you discriminate, you're fired."[3]

By 1998, Denny's had invested so much energy and money in remaking its image that *Fortune* cited them as the second-best company in America for blacks, Hispanics, and Asians in terms of hiring and promotion patterns. Denny's points with pride to the following statistics:[4]

• In 1993, just one Denny's franchise was owned by an African American; today, blacks and other minorities own 36 percent of Denny's 737 franchised restaurants.

• Nearly half of Denny's 50,000-person workforce is now African American, as is one-third of Advantica's management team. The company's twelve-member board of directors has three blacks and one Hispanic.

• Denny's managers and servers are all required to participate in two days of diversity training. At these sessions, they're repeatedly told that every customer must be treated identically—down to the most minute detail. When returning change, for instance, servers are instructed to put the money in diners' hands to avoid implying disrespect.

Despite the pretty numbers and the vast sums of money Denny's has spent attempting to overhaul its image, problems persist on the front lines, where customers come in direct contact with food preparers, servers, and cashiers. These are the *moments of truth* when the public finds out what a company is all about.[5]

Moments of truth are interactions in which a front-line employee effectively becomes the company in the eyes of a customer. These communication events are keys to the success for any company whose bottom line is customer relations.

If, for example, you are treated discourteously by an airline attendant, you are going to take it out on the company. Next time you fly, you will likely choose another carrier. Over the course of time, you'll share your bad experience with friends, relatives, and business associates. If that airline has a long-standing reputation for giving poor treatment to members of certain racial groups, that reputation will become a self-generating negative force.

That's the situation Denny's has continued to battle. The company can institute diversity programs and fire employees for racial insensitivity, but it has learned the hard way that the cumulative effect of too many negative moments of truth can have lasting repercussions.

- In 1999, two Muslims who requested no-pork dishes at a Denny's restaurant in Montana alleged that bacon and ham were intentionally slipped into their meals. The two men filed a discrimination complaint, seeking an apology and $1 million each.[6]
- The same year, a group of thirty black middle school students and their chaperones sued Denny's for racial discrimination, claiming that they were mistreated at a Florida restaurant. The lawsuit asserted that the group had to wait an excessive amount of time to be seated and served. Some members also complained that they received drinks in dirty glasses, including one that appeared to have spit in the bottom.[7]

We can't comment on the veracity of these allegations. However, one of two conclusions (or maybe both) seems apparent:

- Denny's diversity and sensitivity training programs are no substitute for smart racial communication. Even well-intended diversity mandates can backfire. For example, instructing cashiers that they must place change in diners' hands fails to recognize that some groups consider any sort of physical contact offensive or inappropriate.

Diversity programs that tell you to treat everyone the same are not grounded in reality. Effective racial communication is about treating everyone with courtesy—not overlooking differences in background and culture.

• Denny's reputation for bias makes that company a handy target for discrimination lawsuits. Discourteous treatment doesn't always imply racism—even when it happens in the context of a diversity encounter. Still, ours is a litigious society, and there are people and attorneys who look for any excuse to sue. When black customers at Denny's experience second-rate treatment at the hands of white employees, the pattern has been too well established to ignore.

Had the two Muslims been dining in another restaurant, they may have been more inclined to believe that the inclusion of pork in their meals was an accident, not a racist act. When corporate contrition is contradicted by face-to-face discrimination of customers by employees, what are people supposed to think?

SERVE THE BROADEST CUSTOMER BASE

When racially smart companies and entrepreneurs recognize that the needs of a potentially valuable market segment are not being adequately addressed, they seize the opportunity to expand their customer base or create a new market. In some cases, the people stepping in to fill the gaps try to corner the market with their own racial or ethnic group. While there is something to be said for having a sales force that can relate to a particular market segment, it's not necessarily wise for business owners and sales professionals to limit their target audience to members of their own group.

It's true that when African Americans see blacks and other minorities holding responsible positions, they are likely to have a more positive feeling about a company. However, that doesn't mean they will only do business with someone of the same color.

Our research shows that the ability to exercise racial intelligence in sales and customer relations is a more important predictor of success than a person's race or national origin.

All other things being equal, many customers will feel more comfortable buying from someone of the same racial or ethnic group. In most instances, however, all other things aren't equal.

If you can demonstrate that you are more knowledgeable, more customer service oriented, and have more effective communication skills, you can sell successfully to people of any group.

DON'T LET YOUR BIASES—OR THOSE OF YOUR CUSTOMERS—STAND IN THE WAY OF A SALE

We have talked about the futility of trying to alter biases—both your own and those of the people with whom you do business. However, as a salesperson, your one clear goal is to make the sale. Therefore, it would be foolish to allow negative stereotypes to impede the sale—whether they come from you or your customer.

Joe Girard is widely known as "the world's greatest salesman." During one twelve-year period, he sold more retail automobiles than anyone else in the world. Joe is the only salesperson listed in the business section of *The Guiness Book of World Records*.

When we asked Joe Girard to talk about what he learned from his diversity encounters, he emphasized the importance of not allowing racial or cultural bias to get in the way of a sale—even if it's directed at you.

"My real last name is Girardi, which is the name I used when I started selling cars. I was about to close my first sale, when the customer said, 'Girardi, that must be an Italian name.'

"'Actually, my family is from Sicily,' I answered.

"The customer spit on the ground, ripped up his deposit check, and walked out of the dealership.

"From that day on, I began using the last name 'Girard.' And when customers asked, 'What nationality are you?' I would answer, 'What nationality would you like me to be?' More often than not, the strategy worked, and the conversation moved forward."[8]

Was Joe Girard compromising himself by concealing his true ethnicity? Was it wrong of him to become a kind of cultural chameleon? For our money, Joe chose the smartest and most effective strategy.

Joe Girard is a man who quickly understood the goal of his communication, and proceeded in a racially smart fashion. Over the course of his career, Joe sold to people of virtually every race and ethnic group. Any racial preferences or bias he may have harbored were his own business—and he did whatever he could to avoid becoming a catalyst for his customers' prejudices.

WHEN IN ROME, DON'T START RAPPING

There are effective ways for salespeople of all colors to modify the approach Joe Girard used to counter ethnic and racial prejudice. Consider the case of Don Wilson, a thirty-five-year-old African American who earns a six-figure income selling communications products.

When we asked Don to talk about his experiences in diversity encounters, he told us that he often runs into uncomfortable situations because there are so few African Americans in his position. Early in his career, Don felt that being black was a potential impediment to his success. When we asked how he overcame that, Don cited a number of factors.

"One thing that helps me is my name, which is very race-neutral. Plus, there is nothing in the way I speak that identifies me as black. When I contact new clients over the phone, I can tell that they think I'm white. There's no question that I'd have a much harder time getting through the door if people thought I was black. When new clients meet me, I can often tell that they're trying to hide their surprise."

Here's what Don said when we asked how he counsels young African Americans who are thinking about pursuing a career in sales:

"It may sound superficial, but I really believe that one's name is very important. I tell young black men that if I had an Afrocentric name like 'Jamal' or 'Akeem,' I would either change it or use an initial in order to conceal that fact.

"Young men don't always take to this kind of advice. They accuse me of asking them to sell out or hide their 'real selves' by acting and speaking white. I tell them that a salesperson needs to get his foot in the door, and that people are often looking for a reason to deny you entrance.

"If a potential client is white, you'd best assume that race is likely to be used as a conscious or unconscious excuse for that person to say no instead of yes. By presenting yourself in a way that emphasizes a black image, most white customers are likely to feel uncomfortable, and give their business to someone else."

Like other racially smart people, Don has figured out how to negotiate diversity encounters through experience. He was raised in a primarily white neighborhood, and has been relating to white people most of his life. One of the things Don learned going to school and hanging out with white kids was that, in order to feel comfortable, he had to make those around him comfortable.

These early experiences helped Don tear down barriers of potential resistance in the business world. Here is a person who has become adept at dealing with circumstances as they are—not as they should be in a more perfect world.

AVOID USING CODE WORDS

Minorities adapt to the ways of the majority, because that is a reality mandated by numbers. But as people of various colors and ethnicities become a more significant part of the population, it is becoming equally important for whites to know how to talk and act around those of other races and cultures. Consider the following scenario:

A white computer salesman is on the verge of selling a state-of-the-art system to a black customer. The customer is about to take out his checkbook when the salesman asks if he likes basketball.

When the customer answers yes, the white salesman remarks, "Aside from being a great player, that Michael Jordan sure is articulate."

The black customer says he needs to use the men's room and excuses himself. Once out of the salesman's field of vision, he walks out of the store. The salesman finally realizes that the sale has been lost, but he is clueless that the use of the term "articulate" in this context is likely to be interpreted by many blacks as meaning articulate, for a black guy.

Now consider the scenario in reverse: Assume that a white customer said, "Michael Jordan sure is articulate" to a black salesman. In that instance, it would not be in the salesman's interest to respond to such a faux pax. He is there to make the sale—not to train customers in the nuances of racially sensitive language. When profit and productivity are your goals, saying nothing is often the smartest course in the face of racial ignorance.

IF YOU DON'T HAVE ANYTHING PRODUCTIVE TO SAY, SHUT UP!

Carl, a forty-two-year-old black sales manager for an office equipment corporation, was training a group of young sales associates. One of the young white men tried to develop a relationship with Carl by using black slang. This twenty-five-year-old would see Carl in the lunchroom and say things like, "Hey, bro', 'sup?" (Translation: Hey, brother, what's up?) Carl was very put off by this behavior.

"I might use slang in a social situation with some of my African American friends," Carl told us. "But for a white subordinate to use that kind of language is an insult. It's as if he's mocking me by spoofing black stereotypes he's picked up from TV and rap records."

Carl felt the young man had some potential as a sales professional, despite his apparent lack of racial smarts. He also decided that the fellow probably didn't mean to be insulting, and that his behavior was a wrongheaded attempt to make a good impression. Carl explained how he handled the situation:

"I sat down with the young man—tried to talk to him as his supervisor and mentor. I let him know that he could do serious damage to his career by using stereotypes in his interactions with people of other races. I explained that most of the African Americans he'd be dealing with understand that those kinds of stereotypes are bad for business.

"Successful black people don't use that kind of language in the workplace, because it can impede their success. When they're in a business context, they speak and behave in ways that are aimed at inclusion. For a white person to throw out those kinds of stereotypes would be seen as disingenuous at best—blatantly racist at worst."

After that heart-to-heart session with Carl, the young man stopped trying to talk to people in his version of "their language." He found out that when you feel at a loss and have nothing productive to say, the smartest choice is to keep your mouth shut. And if you must say something, don't bring up the issue of race at all.

Make Your Customers Feel Good—About You and Themselves

Many people hate and fear salesmen. That's too bad, because salespeople are an essential bridge between customers and the products and services they need.

When people see a salesman, they see a guy looking to separate them from their money. That's why one of most important things a sales professional needs to do is avoid projecting that stereotypical image. The most effective way to do that is to emphasize the relationship with the customer, rather than the need to get him to place an order.

Jeff, a white high school teacher, related the following incident. "I recently was shopping for a VCR in a local electronics store that promised to beat any advertised price. The African American salesman claimed that he was out of the advertised model. Instead, he tried to sell me a model with fewer features at a higher price. I recognized this as a standard bait-and-switch tactic, and I wasn't going to fall for it in any case.

"I guess the salesman sensed that I was going to walk, and he was desperate to say something convincing. He looked at the VCR, then looked at me and said, 'You'd have to be a fool not to buy this VCR.' At that point, I left the store—never to return."

Technically, this was a diversity encounter, though it's impossible to know what role race played in the salesman's unprofessional behavior. Both parties were certainly aware of the other's race. Nevertheless, Jeff feels strongly that this episode was not about race.

We believe that the basic problem here was a high-pressure salesman who worked for a company that cared nothing about making customers feel good. Such companies will attract a certain amount of business, based strictly on offering the lowest price. However, in today's competitive business environment, customers can usually demand both competitive prices and good customer service.

Jeff described his experience with the electronics salesman as a painful one, which got us to thinking.

Physicians (at least the good ones) feel obliged to ease pain. However, this is not a value that's generally associated with sales and other business dealings. Imagine, then, how effective it would be if sales professionals could find a way to help customers relax— to ease the discomfort that often surfaces in diversity encounters.

Some years ago, there was a bestselling book titled *Swim with the Sharks*. The book contained lots of standard advice, like remembering your customers' birthdays and the first names of their kids. People were intrigued by the book's title, even though the content hardly evoked a shark's killer image. Yet salespeople have traditionally talked about customers in predatory terms, and the movers and shakers in a given industry are often referred to as "killers."

Racially smart customer service involves abandoning the traditional "shark" or "killer" mentality that seeks to exploit the "mark's" vulnerability and weakness. On the contrary, success in diversity encounters hinges on increasing comfort and reducing stress.

The Process in Action: Understanding Your Response Style

It's tough to help customers relax if they sense that you are ill at ease. Diversity encounters often generate tension and stress. Therefore, it's important to recognize the ways they may be affecting your behavior.

Tension is an automatic response that can preclude more productive behaviors. By identifying the feelings that make you feel uncomfortable, you can gain control over the situation—and the way in which others are likely to respond to you.

The flip side of this is becoming sensitive to the stresses and tensions of your customers, and creating an environment that makes both of you feel more comfortable. The following factors can trigger tension in a diversity encounter:

- Negative perceptions of the other person. The chances of success in any sales situation increase when you can establish a collaborative atmosphere between you and the customer. It's up to you to help a customer recognize that there's a mutuality of interests between you. That's not going to happen if you're an African American sales professional who believes that all white people hate blacks, or if you're a white salesperson who thinks most blacks are not very trustworthy.
- Buying into negative stereotypes about yourself. Research reveals that many African American salespeople are "acutely conscious of stereotypic thinking" and that "the issue of race is always present in their interpersonal relations."[9]

When these feelings are carried to an extreme, people will sometimes buy into stereotypes about themselves and act them out. This amounts to a self-fulfilling prophecy—one that has damaging effects on a person's self-esteem and on his effectiveness in sales-oriented diversity encounters.

As you continue to gain perspective on what causes you and your customers to grow tense, you'll be less likely to become argumentative, or to perceive others as holding your race against you. Once your own tension level is reduced, you will be better able to make your customers feel relaxed.

SHARPEN YOUR LISTENING AND OBSERVATION SKILLS

- How does a salesperson know that a customer is distracted by personal problems and needs a sympathetic ear?
- How does a manager know when a team member needs to be encouraged or gently chided?
- How does an entrepreneur know how to keep a client who is considering switching to a competitor?
- How does a job seeker know when to talk and when to listen during an interview?

The key to success in all these communication events hinges on one's ability to pick up on verbal and nonverbal cues. Unless you are attuned to your customers' needs, it will be very difficult to convince them to say yes to your needs.

Effective Verbal Communication: Knowing How to Listen

There is no more important communication skill than listening, yet most people find it much easier to talk. Even when they're not talking, salespeople often carry on internal dialogues that prevent them from hearing what their customers are saying.

Communication is a two-way process, one in which you and the other person are exchanging needs. That's why effective listeners are the most persuasive communicators. Unless you understand your customer's needs, you're not likely to achieve your objective in a sales-oriented situation.

Remember, it ultimately doesn't matter how hard a customer is trying to get a message across if you can't hear what's being said.

As we discussed in the previous section, making people feel good is a key component of successful selling and customer service. Few things provide as much emotional nourishment as the feeling you get when someone is truly hearing what you have to say. Listening to your customers makes them feel valued and increases their desire to do business with you. Unless customers get that sense, they will continue to evaluate you in the following objective terms:

- Am I really interested in what this person has to say or sell?
- Is this person an authority whose word and opinion I respect?
- Do I find this person pleasing and attractive?
- What are the potential consequences of not listening to this person?

Once you help customers get past these questions, they start paying more attention to what you have to say. Here's how the technique works:

Customers perceive that you are listening to them. That makes them feel good, and positively disposed to listen more carefully to you.

This type of mirroring is especially effective in diversity encounters, because it diffuses tensions and minimizes interference from stereotypes and negative predispositions. The following techniques can help you become a better listener:

- If you tend to talk too much, make a determined effort to shut up. This simple change will give customers the space to talk more—while giving you an opportunity to do more listening.
- If you're someone who tends to focus more on your own anxieties than on your customers' needs, practice directing more attention on the other person and less on yourself. Remember, your chances of success increase when customers feel that the interaction centers around them, rather than you.
- When you're alone, write down the thoughts and feelings that stop you from listening to your customers. Ask yourself: How did my lack of listening affect the outcome of the interaction?

Remember, listening habits take years to acquire, so don't expect to change them quickly. The good news is that even a small improvement in your listening skills can make a big difference in the outcome of your dealings with customers.

• Recognize how feelings about racial differences affect your ability to listen. Negative feelings and stereotypes about a customer's race can make it difficult to hear that person. In some cases, these feelings can preclude listening completely. For example, some African Americans we interviewed reported that white salespeople ignore them in car dealerships, computer stores, and other retail outlets.

"It's as if they can't believe that a black person can afford to buy what they're selling," a successful black accountant told us. "As soon as I get that sense, I take my business elsewhere."

Black sales professionals also need to be watchful of stereotypes that can make it difficult to listen. For example, if a black salesman is convinced that a white customer will never buy from him, he might ignore cues that the person is actually eager to make the purchase.

Effective Nonverbal Communication: Understanding Body Language

It should come as no surprise that people don't always say what they think. In the context of diversity encounters, men and women are prone to keep their thoughts close to the vest—and often use words to provide cover—not to convey information. Body language is the silent communication that can help you figure out what's really on someone's mind. Reading and "speaking" this nonverbal language is a powerful tool that can help you achieve your objectives.

Once you become skilled at probing what's behind the spoken word, it becomes easier to motivate people to give you what you want.

Human beings think at roughly 300 to 400 words a minute, and speak at an average of 100 to 150 words a minute. Therefore, information is absorbed at two to three times the rate at which someone is speaking. This time gap translates into opportunities to observe body language, and assess how these cues fit into the total communication picture.

Knowing how to read people can help you sell your products and services, interview and negotiate successfully, and motivate others to help you achieve your business objectives. This skill can also help you figure out whether someone is lying or telling the truth. The other side of the body language coin is understanding and controlling the nonverbal messages you are transmitting.

In every interaction, there are automatic reactions between people that are more likely to come out in gestures than in words. Gestures can reinforce or contradict verbal messages. They can also be used to manipulate people and situations.

- Notice whether your customer is making direct eye contact or avoiding your gaze. In general, a person who looks you directly in the eye is assumed to be forthright and truthful. On the other hand, a person who averts his eyes may be trying to conceal what he's thinking—or to create more distance from a salesperson who is coming on too strong.
- You can gather similar information by watching the way a customer reacts when you ask a question. Is her body position open and relaxed, or tense and withdrawn?
- In general, a person who maintains a relaxed, open bearing when you ask a direct question tends to be forthright and truthful. On the other hand, someone whose body suddenly becomes rigid may be trying to conceal something.
- It's also important to look for signs of tension or nervousness, so that you can help the customer feel more comfortable. A customer who crosses his legs, taps his fingers, or forces laughter during your sales pitch may be signaling nervousness or boredom. But remember, different groups have different body language norms, so it's important not to jump to conclusions on the basis of a single cue.

Felix, a Mexican pharmaceutical salesman, described how signals can get crossed when sales professionals and customers don't understand each other's values.

"When I deal with Latin American customers, there's usually a lot of warmth and conversation about family. We are also pretty physical with each other, and often greet one another by hugging, touching, and sometimes even kissing.

"Early in my career, I used the same approach with all my customers. I soon found out that many white non-Hispanics weren't comfortable with that kind of closeness, and I realized that this approach could quickly kill a sale.

Felix also observed that it takes time for a young Latino salesperson to realize that people who need more personal space aren't being intentionally unfriendly. It's simply a question of recognizing that there are differences between racial and ethnic groups in terms of body language and the need for personal space.

For example, one recent study revealed that British and Australians stand farther apart during their interactions than people of other nationalities. A second study that measured how many times people in different nations touched each other when they talked in public yielded the following results:[10]

- Puerto Rico, 180 times an hour.
- France, 110 times an hour.
- Great Britain, zero times an hour.

Ignorance of these kinds of norms can have a negative impact on both international business dealings and diversity encounters. At the same time, it's impossible to keep track of every group's tendencies and preferences.

In most cases, your best bet is to take the lead from your customers, and not jump to any quick conclusions. If you're uncertain about what a customer in a diversity encounter is communicating, consider maintaining a neutral bearing, using body language sparingly, and responding sensitively to the customer's personal-space preferences.

Nonverbal language is most helpful in situations where direct questions are either inappropriate or unlikely to elicit a candid response. The rules of interpreting body language and other nonverbal clues are well known to people who are skilled in the art of persuasion—and deception. A practiced liar can project a calm demeanor and offer up convincing-sounding laughter at will. This person can look you directly in the eye, promise you the sale, and then never take your phone calls again.

You may also run into scrupulously honest people who are unsophisticated in nonverbal communications. These men and women can give the mistaken impression that they're trying to deceive you, when that's the last thing on their minds.

Jo-Ellan Dimitrius, author of *Reading People* and a jury consultant on many high-profile criminal cases, uses a combination of nonverbal and verbal cues to determine whether a person is telling the truth. She finds that liars fall into several overlapping categories:[11]

- *The occasional liar.* This kind of person prefers to tell the truth. Therefore, he or she feels uncomfortable about the deception. You can pick up that discomfort through body language, tone of voice, and other verbal cues.
- *Frequent or habitual liars.* This type of person is more practiced at covering up, but often loses track of lies and can get sloppy. You should look for inconsistencies between what the person says and what is conveyed through body language.
- *Professional liars* are the most difficult to identify. This type of person lies for a specific purpose, like the salesman who is trying to con a customer into "the deal of a lifetime," or the car mechanic who is practiced at turning a hundred-dollar tuneup into a two-thousand-dollar engine overhaul.

The professional liar has his pitch prepared and memorized in advance. He may offer convincing arguments that can only be disproven by independent sources. When someone seems too slick, consider that a red flag. It's essential to observe the dissonance between a person's body language and the words he or she uses. When these factors are out of sync, there may be something wrong—or you may still need more information to draw an accurate conclusion.

NEGOTIATE TO A CLOSE

The purpose of any productive negotiation is to get what you want, though not necessarily at someone else's expense. In their book, *Getting to Yes*, Roger Fisher and William Ury call a "win-win" negotiation one in which each participant's interests are satisfied. Fisher and Ury suggest the following ways to negotiate terms and resolve conflicts. We have adapted them for use in diversity encounters:[12]

- *Separate personalities from problems.* Focus on the issues at hand. Never resort to personal attacks, just because someone won't give you what you want. If you must attack, direct that aggressive energy toward confronting the issues. Never get personal, especially when you're angry. Be very careful not to say or do anything that appears to disparage a customer's (or business adversary's) race or culture.

- *Focus on common interests—not polarized positions.* Don't allow racial stereotypes and culturally based style differences to interfere with your efforts to achieve mutually beneficial solutions. Make certain that substantive differences in your objectives are not confused with perceived bias and racial anger.

- *Explore as many options as possible in attempting to reach mutually acceptable solutions.* Know what you want—and what you're prepared to give away. Find out what the other person wants, and what he or she is willing to give away. Utilize the effective communication techniques we explored in the previous section to discern as much as you can about the person's limits. Once each of you knows what the other wants—and how far the other person is willing to bend—the process will accelerate.

- *Use objective criteria—not subjective feelings—to make determinations.* Always deal from a position of strength. Steer clear of negative manipulation and browbeating. Don't speak or act in ways that promote stereotypes or foster racial tensions.

- *Never walk out of a negotiation, unless you're truly prepared to kill the deal.* Be aware, however, that you will lose all leverage if the other party senses that you won't walk away—however unsatisfactory the terms.

- *Don't seek total victory.* When one party comes away with total victory and the other feels crushed, the negotiation is not a success. A win-win negotiation requires an outcome that leaves neither party feeling defeated—even if the deal favors one over the other. The need for a double-win is especially important in a diversity negotiation, because hard feelings can exacerbate racial tensions and increase the potential for negative communication.

The Process in Action: Closing the Sale

The *close* has long been thought of as the most important part of the sale. In fact, the question of whether or not a salesperson closes a sale is usually answered by how well the seller executes the previous steps we have detailed in this chapter. If these pre-close elements are in place, the chance of having a successful sales or customer service negotiation increases significantly. However, if one or more of these factors is not properly addressed, you may never have the opportunity to close the deal.

Preparation is the key to successful selling and customer service, and much of it takes place before you ever meet or speak with the prospective customer. An important aspect of that preparation involves understanding the characteristics of your customer base.

As we point out in Chapter Three, most races and cultures share many of the same basic values, though they are often expressed in different ways. For example, people of all races want to be treated honestly and with respect.

People of every race also want to live well, but here, too, this common desire can be manifested in different ways. Some cultures value "saving for a rainy day." Others place more emphasis on "living for today." There are also variations in the way different groups utilize leisure time and define age and gender roles. All these factors can have a significant impact on your customers' buying behavior, and they need to be considered in developing sales and negotiation strategies.

In general, we don't endorse basing behavior in diversity encounters on lists of group characteristics. There are too many differences among people of the same race, and too many different groups with overlapping characteristics.

It's not uncommon, for example, for white and black Americans to mistake a Hindu Indian customer for a Muslim Pakistani, or a Chinese customer for one who is Korean. When you combine these inaccurate guesses with rigid lists of cultural dos and don'ts, you have a surefire formula for a sales disaster.

Once again, our research shows that developing a racially smart operational style is far more useful than memorizing lists of racial and cultural characteristics. Nevertheless, there is something to be said for researching your audience.

For example, if your customers are observant Jews or Muslims, it's useful to know that these religions forbid the consumption of pork. If your customers are strict Hindus, it helps to be aware that their religion forbids eating beef. This kind of specific knowledge can influence everything from developing a new product line to planning the menu for an upcoming business lunch.

WHAT MARKET RESEARCH REVEALS

In developing their campaigns, advertisers need to target specific market segments. The following are some of the "hot buttons" for selling to specific racial and ethnic groups.[13]

MARKETING TO AFRICAN AMERICANS
- Strong on ethnic identity.
- Believe in brand and personal loyalty.
- Value prestige and status.

MARKETING TO HISPANICS
- Strong on traditional family values.
- Place great importance on ethnic holidays and celebrations.
- Appreciate the presence of Spanish-speaking sales staff.

MARKETING TO ASIAN AMERICANS
- Stress product's high quality.
- Dislike sales techniques that downgrade the competition.
- Place great emphasis on preserving dignity and saving face.

Concluding Thoughts

In sales encounters, negative decisions are much easier to make than positive ones. A job interviewer, for example, needs less than a minute to decide against hiring someone. This kind of snap decision is often based on superficial factors, such as a person's dress, hairstyle, or body language. The same principle applies to many other sales situations.

Think about your own experiences as a customer. Saying yes means that you have agreed to invest money and/or time in what the other person is selling, so you need to be convinced. If, however, there's something about that person's presentation that turns you off, you immediately start thinking about a way to end the encounter gracefully.

Race can be an important factor in determining whether or not a sale will be closed. Someone may like you because you share the same culture and ethnicity. The next person may dislike you because of stereotypes or experience-based feelings about members of your particular racial group.

Remember, there are always going to be variables outside your control. Even the most successful sales professionals don't close anything like a 100 percent of their prospective customers. The idea is to do everything possible to increase your odds. When you incorporate the effective sales and customer service techniques we have discussed in this chapter into a racially smart operational style, you will have a powerful tool for increasing the likelihood that your customers will say *yes*!

D E A L I N G   W I T H   T H E
S Y S T E M

May the forces of evil become confused on the way to your house.
—GEORGE CARLIN (COMEDIAN)

At one time or another, we all have encounters with police officers, judges, doctors, school administrators—and a litany of
bureaucrats. We refer to these often unavoidable and sometimes
gut-wrenching pieces of business in our lives as dealing with "the
system." Consider the following scenarios:

- A state trooper of another race pulls you over for speeding,
  though you're not traveling faster than other cars on the road.
- A doctor of another race is about to give you a test that can be more
  or less painful, depending on the amount of pressure he applies.
- A school principal of another race has it in his power to decide
  whether or not your child will be placed in the class of the teacher
  you prefer.

As with all diversity encounters, the way a person deals with the
system is largely a product of experience. In our capitalist society,
socioeconomic status is one important mediator of how people feel
and behave when they interact with representatives of the legal,
medical, and educational systems. Race is another.

Wealthy individuals of all colors can afford the best doctors, hire the best attorneys, and send their children to the best private schools. Nevertheless, there are times when wealth—and even celebrity—cannot overcome racial bias.

In this chapter, we explore the way race mediates some of the most common diversity encounters people have with the system. We show you how to effectively negotiate these often tricky, sometimes dangerous encounters in the following circumstances:

- Confrontations with the police.
- Communications with doctors and health care providers.
- Interactions with teachers and school administrators.

As always, our focus is practical—not political. At the same time, we understand that these issues have a strong political subtext, which makes it impossible to navigate this terrain effectively without some degree of fluency in the underlying politics. Accordingly, we explore the feelings and experiences of white police officers, especially those who patrol primarily black urban neighborhoods. We contrast these with the experiences and feelings of African Americans and Hispanics who feel they've been abused by the police because of their race.

While the ethics of some diversity encounters speak for themselves, we are not interested in taking sides. Our purpose in examining certain opposing viewpoints is to help you understand and negotiate your dealings with the system in a racially smart manner.

PROFILING: THE REAL DEAL

Many of the problems nonwhites have with the system come under the general rubric of profiling. However, it's important to understand how profiling fits into the question of racial discrimination—and human experience in general.

People form ideas and opinions about every encounter. As a person goes through life, he or she develops a kind of shorthand—a way of categorizing individuals according to their characteristics. Many of these opinions are based on quick and superficial impressions about age, body size, dress, grooming, speech, gender—and race.

Advertisers take advantage of this shorthand to sell products. For example, they may have an actor wear glasses in order to convey intellect. In reality, that actor may be functionally illiterate. An advertising agency may employ a muscular actor to create an impression of vigorous health, and the public may never know that he is suffering from heart disease. The agency may have a black actor who is a junior at Yale wear baggy pants and read lines from a rap record. That's not who he is. Still, as far as the public is concerned, he fits the profile of a ghetto tough.

"Stereotyping" is the term that has traditionally been used to describe categories formed on the basis of race. "Profiling"—a more recent variant—describes the expectations that are applied to people of a particular group.

Stereotyping and profiling can result in unfair outcomes, but they are part of the human condition. Instant decisions are often made on the basis of how others feel about your physical characteristics. That is a given in any business negotiation, as well as any encounter with the system.

It would be a mistake to approach any human interaction and assume there is a completely level playing field. In one way or another, profiling and stereotyping always factor into the equation. Consequently, you must take these responses into consideration when assessing every diversity encounter—both from your perspective and that of the other person.

Profiling can be a useful mechanism—when it is used to process information and determine trends. Job applicants, especially those who will be dealing with the public, should always be checked for important background facts—like a past criminal record or prior sexual offenses. (It is surprising how often this is not done.) However, profiling becomes problematic when it leads to some form of discrimination based purely on race. When racial profiling is practiced by police officers, physicians, or school administrators, the results can be devastating.

Racially smart individuals understand their own biases. What is more important, they know how to handle and deflect bias when authorities in the legal, medical, or educational system use racial characteristics to intentionally or inadvertently target them as part of a negative selection process.

DRIVING WHILE BLACK, AND OTHER ROADSIDE TALES

In April 1998, two state troopers patrolling the New Jersey Turnpike fired eleven shots into a van carrying four black and Hispanic men, hitting three of them. Not surprisingly, the troopers and the four men offered conflicting accounts of the incident.

The troopers contended that they ordered the van's driver to pull over to the shoulder of the road, because he was speeding. As the officers approached the stationary van, it went into reverse and struck one of them. After that, both troopers began shooting. The van backed into the patrol car, then drove onto the turnpike and collided with a Honda Accord, which hit the center divider and burst into flames.

According to the troopers' account, the van then drove directly at them. They responded by firing "several rounds from their service weapons at the approaching vehicle." At that point, the van came to a stop on the right shoulder, and the four occupants were removed.

The young men told a very different story. They denied that they were speeding, and claimed that they had put the van into reverse by mistake. As they were trying to get the vehicle under control, the troopers opened fire. Lawyers for the young men contended that the officers pulled the van over because the driver and passengers were "black and brown."[1]

Was the driver of the van speeding, as the troopers claim? Or did the officers stop the vehicle simply because of the hue of the occupants' skin? Only the troopers and the four young men know the truth. Still, every day, blacks and Latinos complain that they are detained—and often harassed—by police solely on the basis of color. This practice has come to be known as racial profiling, or "driving while black."

As with corporate bias, denial is usually the first response of police and other authorities who are accused of acting in a racist fashion. In the case of racial profiling, however, the laws are less clear than those applied to the workplace.

According to the Fourth Amendment, the police cannot detain an individual without some valid reason—or *probable cause*. For example, an officer can stop you if you're speeding or if your car has a broken taillight, but has no right to detain you solely on the basis of race. However, recent decisions by the United States Supreme Court have given police the latitude to use traffic stops as a pretext to fish for evidence of criminal activity. As a recent American Civil Liberties Union (ACLU) report on racial profiling points out:

"Every driver probably violates some provision of the vehicle code at some time during even a short drive, because state traffic codes identify so many different infractions. If the police target a driver for a stop and search, all they have to do to come up with a pretext for a stop is follow the car until they observe the driver making an inconsequential error or technical violation."[2]

African American leaders have been complaining for years that black drivers (especially young black men) are stopped on local roads and state highways far more often than other motorists. And there is no shortage of data and anecdotal evidence demonstrating that the police exercise this discretionary power, mostly against blacks and Latinos.

THE FOURTH AMENDMENT TO THE UNITED STATES CONSTITUTION

The right of the people to be secure in their persons, houses, papers, and effects, against unreasonable searches and seizures, shall not be violated, and no Warrants shall issue, but upon probable cause, supported by Oath or affirmation, and particularly describing the place to be searched, and the persons or things to be seized.

Complaints of racial profiling are pervasive in every area of the country. While some police officers will acknowledge, off the record, that they practice racial profiling, official admissions are rare. When they do occur, controversy and cover-your-behind politics are sure to follow.

In a 1999 newspaper interview, New Jersey state police chief Carl Williams started out by saying that he did not condone racial profiling, but added that it would be "naive" to think that race is not a factor in drug crime. Williams then launched into the following diatribe:

"Today . . . the drug problem is cocaine or marijuana. It is most likely a minority group that's involved with that. . . . If you're looking . . . at heroin and stuff like that, your involvement there is more or less Jamaicans. . . . They aren't going to ask some Irishman to be a part of their [gang] because they don't trust them.

"Two weeks ago, the president of the United States went to Mexico to talk to the president of Mexico about drugs," he added. "He didn't go to Ireland. He didn't go to England."[3]

Any astute politician knows that she or he can't appear to endorse profiling or any other action that can be perceived as racially biased. So it was hardly surprising that New Jersey Governor Christine Todd Whitman promptly fired Williams.

The unceremonious dismissal of Chief Williams, a New Jersey state trooper for thirty-seven years, resonated in police departments throughout the country—many of which were already under fire for stopping and searching motorists strictly on the basis of race.

Governor Whitman, who had defended Williams in the past, still contended that he was "not a racist." Instead, she characterized Williams's remarks as demonstrating "a level of insensitivity that I just couldn't [tolerate]."

Whitman added, "My only desire is to ensure that every person in the state . . . can feel the same sense of confidence and pride in [the police] that I do."[4]

And herein lies one of the essential dilemmas:

Most white people regard the police as protectors of their freedom and safety. Many blacks and Hispanics hate and fear cops, whom they see as violators of their civil rights.

The vast majority of white Americans feel good about their dealings with the police. Many African Americans and Latinos tell upsetting stories of being profiled—by state troopers on the highway, by customs officials at airports, and by officers who patrol the streets and parks.

And what about the cops themselves? Most of the police officers we interviewed condemned racial profiling. But off the record, many characterized the practice as a matter of "following your gut." If a cop can't rely on his own instincts, the argument goes, every citizen suffers—including minorities.

Governor Whitman admitted that she has no problem with police using race as one of several criteria for targeting criminal suspects. Even President Clinton, who condemned the practice of racial pro filing as "morally indefensible [and] deeply corrosive," approved the profiling of Hispanics by Arkansas state police as part of a drug-interdiction program when he was governor in the 1980s. According to an article in the *Washington Times*:

"The Arkansas plan gave state troopers the authority to stop and search vehicles based on a drug-courier profile of Hispanics, particularly those driving cars with Texas license plates. . . . A lawsuit and a federal consent decree ended the practice . . . the next year. . . . Governor Clinton criticized the court's decision and, at one point, threatened to reinstate the program despite the court's ruling.

"Mr. Clinton said then that he considered the searches as [being comparable to] airport metal detectors; that drugs were a bigger problem than airplane safety; [and that he] wished a way could be found to expand the searches again."[5]

Hispanic groups were understandably offended by these revelations, and some leaders questioned the president's "moral authority to lead a national campaign on this issue." Still, it's hard to blame Mr. Clinton, or any politician in his position, for supporting the police—especially when the United States Supreme Court appears to condone their practices.

Certain types of categorizing or profiling are widely accepted in criminology and other social sciences. For example, the Federal

Bureau of Investigation's behavioral science unit has been lauded for developing a criminal profile of serial killers—a profile that happens to have a racial and gender component. Here, the vast majority of serial killers are white males. However, the kind of profiling that targets blacks and Latinos raises other daunting questions:

• Is it in our interest for the legal system to classify people and their likely behaviors on the basis of race, so that potential criminals can be identified?

• Does the use of categories that contain a racial component threaten the public good, since a certain percentage of innocent people will inevitably be misclassified?

Here again, the answer depends on whom you ask. A white person who fears nonwhites may not care if innocent blacks and Hispanics get caught in the net—just so long as he and his family are protected. The picture looks a lot different to a black person—who may feel that no amount of success and wealth shields him from a police force and a legal system that perceives him as a potential bad guy.

Unlike the four young men who were shot in their van on the New Jersey Turnpike, most middle- and upper-class black targets of racial profiling are stopped and then let go unharmed, often without even being issued a summons. Nevertheless, there are more than enough cases of innocent African Americans being searched, abused—and occasionally shot—by police to make the black community wary and cynical about the legal system.

Even Christopher Darden, the African American prosecutor in the O. J. Simpson criminal case—who some people feel was used by the white legal system to sell out his own people—reports that he is frequently stopped by law enforcement officers.

Darden, who spent fourteen years working closely with Los Angeles police to prosecute accused criminals, understands that society's interests in fighting crime need to be balanced "against the rights of the individual to be safe and . . . not to be bothered by the police. But the scale is tipped totally in favor of the police and totally in favor of suspending the rights of those of us who supposedly fit the profile. It's unfair and it's wrong."

Darden talks about the rules of how a black man is supposed to act when he is stopped by the police—rules that many fearful African American and Hispanic parents pass on to their children:

"Don't move. Don't turn around. Don't give some rookie an excuse to shoot you. . . . If the police stop you for no apparent reason at all, what's to stop them from . . . physically harming you for no reason at all?"[6]

"White parents worry about their kids getting into an accident," the African American mother of a nineteen-year-old son told us. "I worry that he'll mouth off to an officer or make a wrong move, and end up getting beaten—or killed."

It's understandable that many nonwhite people feel frustrated and angry about the situation. Every law abiding, taxpaying citizen is entitled to equal protection of the law, regardless of race. Nobody has a right to harass drivers on the highway or pedestrians who are walking down the street. If an officer does stop you, he is obliged to treat you with respect. However, the individual motorist needs to know how to behave, if he or she is profiled.

WHAT *NOT* TO DO IF YOU ARE THE TARGET OF RACIAL PROFILING

- *Don't argue the Fourth Amendment.* If you believe that a police officer has violated your rights, you can contact the ACLU or file a complaint with his superior officer at a later time. If the circumstances warrant, you can even take your case to court. However, at the point you are stopped, it's important to maintain control of your emotions and your behavior.
- *Don't be sarcastic or condescending to the officer. Always* be cooperative and polite.
- *Don't display anger—even if it's justified.* Most police officers resent challenges to their authority, and may overreact to any real or perceived affront.
- *Don't lose sight of your goal.* The objective in most racial-profiling scenarios is to end the encounter as quickly as possible with a minimum of potential trauma. Getting stopped for no good reason

is inconvenient. But being jacked up against your car and searched is an experience that can stay with you for years. Getting handcuffed and taken into custody escalates the nightmare.

Remember, racial intelligence is about acting on the basis of what makes sense, rather than acting on the basis of emotion—even if the emotions you are experiencing are justified and powerful. As we point out in Chapter Three, the only way to determine whether a behavior is racially intelligent is to ask yourself the following question:

Is my response likely to help me become more effective in realizing my goal?

Racial profiling by police is a reality in a system that often treats minorities unfairly. However, the immediate issue isn't fairness. Rather, it's your ability to negotiate the encounter you are facing at the time.

How to Handle Diversity Encounters with the Police

Consider the way Howard, a forty-one-year-old African American, deals with being stopped on the highway. Howard is a teacher who works two jobs to support his wife and four children. One of his jobs requires a sixty-mile drive from his home along the New Jersey Turnpike, where he almost always goes at speeds that exceed the usual eight-to-ten-mile-an-hour flex that most drivers take for granted.

Keep in mind that this is a highway where blacks often complain about being stopped for suspicion of transporting or possessing drugs and firearms—even when they're not speeding. Yet Howard, who generally goes seventy-five in a fifty-five-mile-per-hour zone, has found an effective way to deal with local police and state troopers.

"In the first place, I drive a four-year-old Toyota Camry, which is about as generic and low-profile a car as there is. I'm a dark-skinned black guy, going twenty miles over the speed limit, so I'd have to be crazy to call any more attention to myself. Considering the speed at which I drive, it's surprising that I'm not stopped even more often. I have received some tickets over the years, but all of them were justified."

Howard told us that he always acts polite and deferential when he's stopped, and that he has never been searched or suffered any abuse at the hands of police. Through experience, he has learned how to talk to law enforcement officers in a way that turns the encounter in his favor.

"I've become aware of the kind of body language police like," Howard told us. "For example, I always keep my hands in plain sight, and ask if it's okay to remove my license and registration from the glove compartment. But the first thing I do is acknowledge that I was speeding, and apologize.

"I always address a state trooper as 'Trooper' rather than 'Officer,' because I've learned that this is what they like to be called. I then explain that I work two jobs that are far away from each other, and that I need to get to and from work quickly.

"I explain that I can't afford any more points on my driver's license, and ask the trooper if he'd consider issuing a ticket for a lesser offense—one that wouldn't add additional points. The (mostly white) troopers almost always agree not to give me a speeding ticket. They either write a ticket for a lesser offense or a warning. Sometimes they just tell me to slow down—and let me be on my way."

Howard went on to tell us that, sometimes, the troopers begin to relax, and engage him in small talk. On one such occasion, Howard said to the trooper, "I hope you and I can meet under more pleasant circumstances."

"Why?" the trooper responded. "This isn't so unpleasant."

Some may characterize Howard's dealings with the police as demeaning, but we see his approach as a highly effective way of handing a potentially volatile situation.

Even the most bigoted individuals will generally acknowledge that there are "a few good ones" in any racial group. Howard's conduct makes it abundantly clear that he is the antithesis of any negative stereotypes an officer might harbor about African

Americans. Once those stereotypes collapse, the trooper's initial suspicions get reframed in the following way:

"This guy isn't a drug dealer or any other kind of criminal. Actually, he's a lot like me—a hardworking family man, doing his best to make ends meet."

At this point, Howard has effectively seized control of the situation, and the troopers are usually happy to give him what he wants. Consider the seamless way in which Howard works the racial intelligence process we lay out in Chapter Three:

Step 1. Figure out what's in it for you. Howard understands that, as a black motorist, he is vulnerable to racial profiling. His speeding makes it more likely he will attract attention. Howard has no control over his color, and he's decided that speeding is something he needs to do. To offset these factors, Howard has made a conscious decision to drive a low-profile car—and to figure out the best way to communicate effectively with the officers that stop him.

Step 2. Don't pretend to be color-blind. Howard recognizes that the state troopers are mostly white, and that they may be predisposed to look at African American males in a negative way. He is well aware that these roadside stops are inherently not race-neutral, and can easily spin out of control if not handled effectively.

Step 3. Watch, but don't preach. Howard has carefully listened to and observed the way the police officers interact with him. He knows all about the horrible experiences some black drivers have encountered. Nevertheless, he doesn't believe that all police and state troopers are racist. Instead, he tries to listen and look at the way troopers act and speak, so that he can communicate with them more effectively.

Step 4. Build on what all of us share. Howard recognizes that he has a great deal in common with police officers. Like him, cops have jobs to do and families they love. Most would rather have a pleasant interaction than one filled with conflict.

Step 5. Learn from every experience. Howard has used all of his encounters with the police to monitor his own feelings, and to learn as much as possible about the mind-set of a typical police officer. For example, since he found out that state troopers have an especially positive response to being addressed as "Trooper," he always makes it a point to refer to them in that manner.

Step 6. Look at it through the other person's eyes. Howard understands that the police have a difficult and dangerous job to do. He goes out of his way to make the interaction as congenial as possible for the officers, and consequently, for himself.

Step 7. Know what you want to accomplish. Ask yourself: What do I want to get out of this interaction? Howard is totally clear about his objective: He wants to convince the officer not to issue a speeding ticket, and he never loses sight of that goal.

Step 8. Close the deal. Generate a response that is most likely to help you achieve your objective. Everything Howard says and does in his encounters with police is in the service of his goal. As a result of becoming racially smarter, his stops on the highway almost never result in speeding tickets, although he is the first to admit that he deserves them.

Howard has essentially found a way to turn the tables. It is now *he* who is taking the initiative and profiling the police officer. In so doing, Howard is addressing both his business and personal objectives: to arrive at work in a timely manner without receiving a speeding ticket.

DEALING WITH BLACK POLICE: DOS AND DON'TS FOR WHITE MOTORISTS

White motorists (at least those who present a relatively "normal" appearance) are rarely targeted by police because of their race.

However, the numbers of minority police officers are growing, so a racially smart white person needs to be cognizant of a few basic guidelines to avoid getting trapped.

While race is always a factor in any diversity encounter, most black and other minority officers see themselves as cops first. Therefore, these are encounters in which a white person should avoid bringing up race at all. In this context, the following rules apply:

• *Don't use the other person's slang or inside language.* Speak in your normal manner and tone of voice. Don't try to ingratiate yourself to a Hispanic officer by breaking into Spanish, or to an African American officer flaunting your version of black slang. This approach is likely to poison an otherwise innocuous situation.

• *Don't risk having your words misinterpreted.* If you want to engage the officer in light conversation, don't talk about your favorite African American basketball player or jazz musician.

• *Show respect.* Never forget that a police officer is in the power position during any encounter on the street or highway. This does not give him the right to disrespect or abuse you. However, it's important to demonstrate a fitting amount of deference to his or her authority.

DO COPS HATE RACIAL MINORITIES?

Of all the real and alleged incidents of police brutality against African Americans, few have generated as much public outrage as the 1991 beating of an ex-convict named Rodney King by four Los Angeles policemen. The incident was captured on videotape by a resident of a nearby apartment. The tape lasted just over a minute, and was broadcast on American television more often than almost any other video in history. Over the ensuing years, it has become an indelible part of the nation's collective memory.

To many African Americans, the Rodney King beating stands as proof of the hatred white police officers harbor for minorities.

When those four officers were acquitted by an all-white jury, there were riots in south-central Los Angeles, riots that some black leaders justified with the slogan, "No justice, no peace."

Still, what did the Rodney King video prove? That white Los Angeles police officers were racists who enjoy beating on blacks? To some, the video was an indictment of police all over the country.

There have been many other incidents of police brutality since Rodney King. Some of these abuses have been perpetrated against citizens with no criminal record, who, unlike King, did not engage the cops in a pursuit on freeways and city streets at speeds reaching 115 miles an hour.

Maybe it's because of the tape's graphic nature, or the sense that officers were enjoying themselves as they clubbed and used a stun gun to make the 250-pound man submit. Whatever the reason, this incident continues to resonate each time another act of police brutality hits the news—reinforcing the notion that white cops hate African Americans.

"When black people . . . see a police car approaching, they don't know whether justice will be meted out or whether judge, jury and executioner is pulling up behind them," California assemblyman Chris Tucker was quoted as saying at a hearing on LAPD practices following the Rodney King incident.[7]

The question stands: Are police officers looking to do violence to African Americans? No, says Dr. Beverly Anderson, a Washington, D.C., psychologist who specializes in treating officers in the wake of violent incidents and other job-related stresses.

"Most police officers don't grow up in families where they're systematically taught to hate blacks—or any other racial group," Dr. Anderson observes. "For the most part, their reactions are the product of learned behavior—or what psychologists call 'stimulus generalization.'

"People respond emotionally to experiences—especially ones that are traumatic. In a city like Washington, where many of the officers have had violent encounters with African Americans, you can expect them to generalize to others of that racial group."[8]

A 1998 examination by the *Washington Post* seems to support

Dr. Anderson's contention that police violence is not primarily about race. The paper reported that even though Washington has a predominantly black police force and a predominantly black population, the city's cops had one of the highest rates of gun discharges. Meanwhile, New York's police force, which underrepresents minorities, had one of the lowest.[9]

A study of citizen complaints in a number of large cities, including New York, revealed that allegations of excessive police force are more likely to occur against officers of the same race or gender.[10]

Dr. Anderson explains that incidents like the Rodney King beating are the result of inadequate training and a kind of burnout. Police officers have no way of knowing what's in store even in the most routine traffic stop or domestic complaint. "After enough horrible experiences, they often become hypervigilant."

Cal, a Washington, D.C., policeman we interviewed, had stopped to help a hearing-impaired pedestrian on a busy urban street when a black youth appeared out of nowhere and fatally shot his partner. These are tragic events that sometimes happen to police officers, just as cops can sometimes wind up beating—and even killing—an innocent citizen when a routine encounter takes an unexpected turn. That's why it's so important never to test a police officer's patience or challenge his authority in a face-to-face interaction.

It's always important to be aware of who has the power. On the street, or the highway, or in a police station, the officer is in the power position. It's interesting, in this context, to consider Cal's response to the Rodney King incident—a response that was echoed by other police officers we interviewed.

"At first, I was appalled by the way they were beating the guy. But later, as I looked at the tape and found out he'd assaulted an officer, I couldn't believe that the SOB wouldn't go down. Man, he was being tasered with a stun gun that can knock out an elephant. He must have been high on something.

"One other thing: When you're in a car chase, the adrenaline is pumping something fierce. A guy puts you through that, you just might hit him when he finally surrenders. I'm not saying it's right, but you're flying on adrenaline, and it's a very natural thing to do.

"Someone makes you chase him all over town at a hundred miles per hour. Then, suddenly, he stops, walks out of the car and says, 'I give up.' Under the circumstances, a lot of cops will say, 'The hell you give up,' and kick him right in the chops.

"In the academy, they teach you to handcuff the suspect as soon as he's apprehended. The book says that you have no right to lay a hand on him. People expect you to be Robocop, but it's not that easy to turn off your emotions. Everybody on the street knows how it works: If you run from the cops and get caught, there's a good chance you'll get your ass kicked. White, black, it doesn't matter."

DO DOCTORS GIVE BLACK PATIENTS SECOND-RATE TREATMENT?

"I believe doctors are no more or no less racist than anyone else in our society," observes Michelle van Ryn, a medical researcher at the State University of New York, Albany.[11] That may be a true statement, but unfortunately, the biases of doctors and other health care providers can be every bit as lethal—and far more insidious—than a policeman's gun.

Medical students learn basic interviewing techniques, but most of them have virtually no training in how to deal with people on a fundamental human level. In this era of managed care and HMOs, patient complaints and lawsuits against doctors are at an all-time high. The average physician is overburdened, has little time or inclination to listen to patients—which is a critical part of the diagnostic process—and often believes that his or her technical skills obviate the need to look at each patient as an individual.

At our medical school, the two of us jump all over students when we hear them refer to patients as numbers or diseases ("that cancer patient in room 202") rather than by name. But we know that this goes on—even among skillful veteran practitioners. Patients are very sensitive to this impersonal approach, and that serves to exacerbate an increasingly cynical view of physicians—and the health care system in general.

It doesn't help when a high-profile study conducted by the Institute of Medicine reveals that surgical errors, misdiagnoses, and drug mix-ups kill up to 98,000 people annually—and that's just in hospitals.[12]

This is an issue that few doctors are willing to discuss openly, thus creating what the study termed a "culture of silence." One reason for this is fear of lawsuits or punishment by the state medical licensing boards. But Dr. Lucian Leape, a Harvard Medical School professor who studies medical error, offers another explanation.

"Physicians are taught that it's [their] job not to make a mistake," Leape observes. "It's like a sin . . . a moral failing [that] is deeply ingrained in medicine, and it is very destructive."[13]

If physicians aren't willing to admit mistakes that are the product of human error, what are the chances they can face up to mistakes caused by racial bias? This quandary is at the root of why the culture of silence may be more pervasive in the way racial attitudes affect medical treatment of African Americans and other minorities. Doctors are embarrassed to discuss their mistakes publicly, but at least they can evaluate these errors privately in peer-review sessions and, hopefully, learn from them.

On the other hand, we know very few physicians who would admit they have a racist bone in their body—and even fewer who would entertain the thought that their racial attitudes factor into the way they practice medicine. Nevertheless, a growing body of research reveals that doctors' treatment of black patients is influenced by the following attitudes and beliefs:[14]

- *Stereotypes based on race and socioeconomic status.* White doctors who've had little or no experience with African Americans sometimes buy into stereotypes of ghetto life that they've picked up from the media. They sometimes assume, for example, that blacks are uneducated, poor, sexually promiscuous, and prone to abusing drugs.

  "Hardiness" is another stereotype that can factor into the substandard treatment black patients sometimes receive. The "hardiness" stereotype plays into the racist notion that African Americans can tolerate pain better than whites. In the past, this myth resulted in some racially ignorant (and bigoted) white physicians doubling the strength of X rays they administered to blacks because of the fallacious belief that they had thicker skin or bones than Caucasians.

Thankfully, we've come a long way since the days when doctors used racial genetics as a basis for treatment programs. Now arguments about bias are often reframed in terms of socioeconomic status. However, doctors with limited racial intelligence often extend "ghetto" stereotypes to middle-class and well-to-do blacks. As a result, they may believe that any black patient who claims to be in pain is just looking to get drugs, so they wind up not prescribing the most effective course of treatment.

* *Insensitivity to predictable discomfort.* A white doctor may run a practice in which patients are kept waiting—regardless of their race. He or she may have a curt manner, or demonstrate poor listening skills when patients complain or ask questions. No patient wants a rude or inconsiderate doctor. However, black and other minority patients are likely to feel especially vulnerable when dealing with this kind of behavior.

Only 4 percent of physicians in the United States are African American, which means that many black people may never have dealt with a doctor of their own race. To men and women in this position, an uncaring white doctor can become emblematic of a white system that cares nothing about them.

* *Disingenuous claims of "color-blindness."* As we discuss in Chapter Four, we are highly skeptical of people who make the following kinds of statements: "I don't care if a person is black, white, brown, purple, or green. Color makes absolutely no difference to me."

We find that people who say such things have trouble reconciling their true feelings with their intellectual beliefs. The fact is, differences in skin color and ethnic background cannot be ignored—in medicine and in most other contexts.

It is a fact that African Americans are more vulnerable to certain serious diseases than members of other racial groups, and less vulnerable to others. All population groups have predilections for certain illnesses. Doctors who refuse to take these epidemiological factors into consideration because of political correctness do their patients a great disservice. However, a physician can never assume that a given patient does or does not have a certain condition because she's Puerto Rican, Italian, or Chinese.

Black patients may be less trusting of the advice and treatment options doctors recommend—and more wary of the health care system in general. Who can forget the monstrous, federally funded Tuskegee experiment in which black men with syphilis were left untreated for up to forty years because government doctors wanted to study the course of the disease?

Under the circumstances, it's hardly surprising that blacks are less likely to trust doctors, and more likely to seek alternatives to traditional medicine. Even AIDS is seen in some minority communities as a result of a white conspiracy.

• *Cultural ignorance.* Each racial and cultural group has its own standards and norms. For example, the customary age for a first pregnancy varies from one group to another—as does the average number of children in a family.

Health care professionals sometimes overlook a key component of the racial intelligence process, namely, not interpreting the behavior of others based on one's own background and cultural values. When doctors fail to recognize that a patient's choices and actions have a reasonable basis in that person's own culture and experience, the resulting advice and medical treatment can lead to disaster.

The above factors go a long way in explaining why African Americans and other minorities do not get equal treatment from the medical system. Consider the following findings:

• Complaints by black patients are taken less seriously. A study reported in the *New England Journal of Medicine* revealed that doctors were 40 percent less likely to order sophisticated cardiac tests for blacks who complained about chest pain than for whites with identical symptoms.[15]

• Blacks get less intensive treatment. Even though blacks die of coronary heart disease at a higher rate than whites, black patients receive cardiac bypass operations and other advanced procedures about one-fourth as often as whites.

• Blacks are more likely to receive mutilating surgery—even when less severe or invasive alternatives are available. A survey by *Newsday* found that blacks with diabetes are more likely to have their feet or legs amputated, while whites in a comparable condition are more likely to receive surgery designed to restore blood flow and save their legs.[16]

• African Americans with serious kidney disease wait longer for transplants, and are less likely to receive a donor kidney than whites.

• Black patients who suffer from emotional problems are less likely than whites to be referred for psychotherapy. When they are referred, African Americans are more likely to be sent to inexperienced therapists and given more prescription drugs.

• Blacks are less likely than whites to get lung cancer surgery during the early stages of the disease. Consequently, they are more likely to die from a potentially curable condition.

When most doctors are confronted with the disparities in medical care for whites and blacks, they either refute the reliability of the evidence or blame the patient. Yet, the majority of the studies from which the above data were gathered were controlled for factors other than race. The findings are supported by our own observations, as well as a glut of anecdotal material. And while some apologists cite statistics indicating that blacks smoke more, are more prone to obesity, are less likely to seek early medical treatment, and are less able to bear the costs, we think the problem has more to do with a lack of effective racial communication skills on the part of physicians.

HOW CAN HMOs BECOME MORE RACIALLY RESPONSIVE?

• Seek the most diverse group of health care professionals available. As much as possible, create a staff that reflects the racial and cultural diversity of the community the organization serves.

- If a significant number of the patients speak a particular foreign language, attempt to hire at least some staff who are conversant in that language. If this is not feasible, consider hiring a translator whose sole function is to interpret language as well as the cultural customs of the patient population.
- Hold regular staff meetings with the purpose of discussing diversity issues. Invite members of the community to participate and express their concerns. Encourage an open dialogue, where participants can ask questions and offer suggestions.
- Encourage all staff members to develop effective racial communication skills. Require participation in courses, seminars, and other training opportunities, to ensure that these skills and competencies are maintained.

OVERCOMING THE MEDICAL SYSTEM'S RACIAL INEQUITIES

It's long past time for doctors and the medical community to begin addressing a problem that black activist Al Sharpton has called "the new civil rights battle of the twenty-first century." While we wait for that to happen, patients must take matters into their own hands if they want to receive quality treatment from doctors and other health care personnel.

Doctors sometimes see themselves as godlike figures, and interpret questions as challenges to their authority. All physicians have an obligation to communicate effectively to patients. When those communication events are diversity encounters, racial intelligence is a necessary skill. The sad fact is that many doctors have trouble communicating with people of their own culture, and are hopelessly lost when they try to communicate with people from other cultures. If you want to maximize your chances of getting the best available health care, we strongly suggest that you take the following proactive steps:

- *Shop around.* If possible, ask people you trust for referrals to physicians with whom they've had good experiences. Even the best doctors sometimes make mistakes. Nevertheless, a physician's reputation in the community—particularly among people of similar backgrounds—is a factor that merits your consideration.

- *Become an informed consumer.* From the doctor's point of view, you are one of many patients he or she treats in the course of a day. Many doctors don't feel they have time to discuss each patient's medical needs. Others simply have lousy communication skills, and expect patients just to follow orders.

Remember, it's up to you to take responsibility for your own health—and that of your loved ones. If your doctor suggests a diagnosis or treatment plan, demand a thorough explanation. Do some independent research. If what you read is at odds with the information your physician provides, ask for a detailed explanation. Put your questions in writing, so that you don't forget them.

Seek out an independent second opinion for any diagnosis that isn't routine. Second opinions are a must whenever surgery is recommended. If a physician attempts to discourage you from soliciting another doctor's advice, take your business elsewhere.

- *Don't stand for stereotyping.* Most white doctors aren't overt racists. However, that doesn't mean they don't inadvertently allow stereotypes to influence their diagnosis. For example, hypertension, or high blood pressure, is found more frequently and in more severe forms in blacks than in whites. Consequently, a physician might deem a particular blood-pressure level acceptable in an African American that he might consider too high in a white person.

A physician is supposed to take into account a variety of factors in interpreting a patient's blood-pressure reading. These include medical history, family history, and situational anxiety, in which a patient's blood pressure can go up simply because a doctor is examining him.

If you suspect that a physician is using stereotypes to make a diagnosis, confront the problem immediately. As much as possible, speak to the doctor in his own language. Don't expect doctors of a different race to understand or respond positively to your slang and inside speech. You have an investment in getting your doctor to like and respect you, and it's important to keep that goal in sight. Still, communication is a two-way street. If a doctor seems unresponsive or continues to use stereotypes, switch to someone else.

- *Demand plain-English explanations.* Doctors sometimes need to be reminded that patients may not be fluent in medical terminology, even though they're perfectly intelligent in every other way. Communication problems can be difficult enough in any diversity encounter. Doctors who use medical jargon don't make things any easier.

It's important not to allow physicians to intimidate you with technical or scientific language. Sometimes a little humor can go a long way. If, for example, a doctor tells you that you have systemic lupus erythematosis, try saying something like, "Can you try saying that in English for me, Doc?"

- *Trust your gut feelings.* As much as possible, try to work with doctors you feel are trustworthy and caring. If a physician's personal approach strikes you the wrong way, look for someone else.

As we discussed in Chapter Six, doctors are ultimately in the business of customer service, and you are the customer. If you feel you're not being treated with respect, make the doctor comprehend that you will not stand for it. If he still doesn't respond, find another doctor.

- *Don't limit yourself to doctors of your own race.* Many people find that they are most comfortable with people of their own racial group—especially when it comes to something as personal and critical as medical care. The medical profession is becoming more aware of the need for diversity, but who can afford to wait for that to become a reality?

The chances are 96 out of 100 that any given doctor will not be African American. In any event, we strongly suggest that you don't choose a physician solely on the basis of race. The main attributes to look for are superior ability, a commitment to healing, and a respect for patients.

DEALING WITH BLACK DOCTORS: DOS AND DON'TS FOR WHITE PATIENTS

Patients of all colors have plenty of complaints about doctors and the health care system, aside from those that center around racial bias. For the most part, the techniques we've described for overcoming racial inequities are relevant for people of all races and cultural groups. However, there is one special circumstance that needs to be considered.

Black doctors account for only 4 percent of physicians in America, but these numbers are growing—as are those of physicians from other racial and cultural backgrounds. Consequently, there is an increasing probability that white patients will be seeing a minority physician—perhaps for the first time.

With more people belonging to HMOs and managed-care facilities, it's often difficult to select a particular doctor. If the practitioner happens to belong to a different racial group, you may find yourself negotiating an unfamiliar kind of diversity encounter. Consider the scenario in Question 5 of the RQ Test:

You are a <u>white parent</u> taking your sick child to a pediatrician assigned by your new health maintenance organization (HMO). You walk into the examination room to find that the doctor is black. You have no experience with African American doctors, and you're not especially comfortable with the prospect.

What do you do?
   a. Be pleasant and don't respond to the doctor's color. Allow him to examine your child. Who knows? You may like this doctor.
   b. Find some pretense to leave. Walk out of the office. Inform your HMO that you will only accept a white doctor.
   c. Congratulate the doctor for getting so far in life. Tell him that he sets a good example for other blacks to follow.
   d. Tell the doctor nobody in your immediate family has ever had a black physician before. Admit that you feel a little nervous about his examining your child.
   e. Walk out without offering an explanation.

Response *c* is the least racially smart choice. It communicates that you buy into racial stereotypes, and strongly hints that there are things you aren't saying that are even more biased. A variant of this response is: "He's a black doctor—but he's good."

Response *d* is marginally better than *c*, only because at least it is a direct expression of genuine feelings, rather than a recitation of rote stereotypes. Nevertheless, this is still a poor choice, because you gain nothing by bringing up the issue of race.

Responses *b* and *e* are smarter than *c* and *d,* even if they are tantamount to confessions of racial bias. You are entitled to work with a physician with whom you feel comfortable. If the doctor's race is that much of an issue for you, you have a right to refuse. Response *b* is more palatable than *c*, because it calls less attention to what you're doing, and it is more likely to result in your HMO honoring your request. However, both responses would be totally senseless if your child required immediate medical attention.

Response *a* is clearly the smartest way to go. A person's race tells you nothing about his or her level of skill. For all you know, the African American physician is excellent, while the white doctor next door may be a hack. After the initial visit, you can evaluate the doctor using criteria more relevant than race.

RACIALLY SMART WAYS TO DEAL WITH THE EDUCATIONAL SYSTEM

Two first graders whose abilities were later judged to be equal were given different assessments of their academic potentials. Little Johnny's parents were told that he was a brilliant child who was going to do very well in school. Meanwhile, little Bobby's parents were informed that he was a slow learner who would need extra help.

Not surprisingly, Johnny did very well throughout his elementary school career, while Bobby struggled to maintain average grades.

Both of these boys were white. Nevertheless, this experience demonstrates the potential impact of expectations on school performance. In recent years, there have been a number of studies indicating that African American and Hispanic students don't score as well on standardized tests as their white and Asian counterparts. In some of the studies, socioeconomic factors played no apparent role in the results.

Here's the question: Are there fundamental differences in the academic abilities of children of different races, or are the disparities the product of expectations that become self-fulfilling prophecies?

It is not our intent to enter into this hotly contested (and highly political) debate. However, it is important to recognize the glaring features of what some have termed the "achievement gap" in order to develop effective counter-strategies. The following statistics are culled from a variety of studies of racially diverse schools around the country:[17]

THE ACHIEVEMENT GAP

• Black and Latino parents have less access to administrators and teachers.

• White parents are given tours of schools far more often than black or Latino parents.

• White parents are given access to information about gifted and other accelerated programs that is often withheld from their black and Hispanic counterparts.

• White parents are more successful at prodding school bureaucracies to address their children's needs.

• African American children are disciplined at a higher rate than whites, especially in high school.

• Black and Hispanic children are more likely to encounter subtle biases based on group expectations. These disparities affect recommendations for special education, advanced classes, remedial courses, and disciplinary measures.

As with profiling in the legal and medical systems, there is obviously a great deal of work to be done to make public schools more equitable. We heartily encourage you to become involved in changing these systems, through personal effort and community involvement. Parental pressure has caused some districts to examine these disparities, and to address them by hiring more minority teachers, making diversity part of the core curriculum, and requiring educators to take cultural-competency courses.

Unfortunately, school systems tend to be bureaucratic and slow to change. If you have a child in school, the most effective strategy is to become an advocate for that boy or girl. This entails taking the following steps:[18]

1. Make an appointment with the school principal to tour the building and observe classes in session. Principals will sometimes claim they are too busy, but responding to parents is part of their job.

Ask the principal to accompany you on the tour. Spend time in several classes. See if the children appear to be happy and involved in meaningful work. Observe the way the teacher interacts with the class. Ask the principal about the racial diversity of both the curriculum and the educational staff.

This step serves two key purposes: It allows you to draw your own conclusions about the school, and it lets the principal know that you will be proactive in demanding your (and your child's) rights.

2. Attend all meetings where parents are invited, including parent-teacher organizations and board of education meetings. Feel free to ask questions, and don't be intimidated. Remember, when it comes to your child's schooling, *you* are the customer.

3. Stay informed. Look for information about your school published in regional newspapers. Statistics usually include average number of children per class, average teacher's salary, number of dollars spent per pupil, number of teachers with advanced degrees. Find out about the diversity breakdown of students and educational staff—and how both are performing.

To round out the picture, talk to neighbors and others with school-age children. Ask the following questions in an informal way:

- What are the school's strong and weak points?
- Are the children happy?
- Are there specific teachers to seek out or stay away from?
- How effective is the principal and other administrators in maintaining order and high academic standards?
- Are there noticeable differences in the way children of different races are treated?

4. Try to pick your child's teachers. A grown-up's feelings about education are often based on experiences with one or more influential teachers. Successful African Americans have often ruminated about supposedly well-meaning grade school teachers who said things like, "Forget about law school, honey, you're going to work with your hands." However, a single inspirational teacher can turn a child's life around.

Brent Staples, a distinguished black journalist with a Ph.D. in psychology, credits his success to a white English teacher who prodded him to apply to college. Staples had been taking a commercial course in high school, and never even considered college as an option.[19]

If teachers can have so much influence on a child's life, does it make sense to accept a class assignment that's usually made on a more or less random basis? Most school principals cringe at the thought of parents coming to their office or demanding that their child get a particular teacher. That's understandable—but it's not your problem.

Your objective in the situation is to place your child in the best available learning situation. At the very least, you want to avoid teachers who are known to be incompetent, or who give second-rate treatment to children of particular racial groups.

It's a good idea to talk to various teachers, but the most accurate way to judge is to sit in on all the classes in your child's grade level for an hour or more. Then go to the principal's office and express your preferences. The principal may not grant all your requests. However, school administrators do not want to deal with unhappy parents every day, and they will often try to placate such "pains in the neck."

5. Bring up race when it's to your advantage. School districts are designed to deal with hundreds or thousands of students. If your child has a learning disability or some other special need, take advantage of all available services, and make sure they are being offered on a nondiscriminatory basis. Similarly, if you feel that your child qualifies for a gifted or accelerated program, make those feelings known.

Look into the qualifications for those programs, and try to make an honest assessment of how your child stacks up. If you feel he or she is being unjustifiably left out, don't be afraid to ask about the racial breakdown of those classes. It sometimes happens that the mere implication of racial discrimination can tilt the scale in your favor.

GETTING INTO COLLEGE: SHOULD YOU PLAY THE RACE CARD?

James, a thirty-nine-year-old African American attorney, related the following experience. "I graduated from high school second in my class, and was president of the honor society during my junior year. Still, I'll never forget what some of my white classmates said when I was accepted to Columbia University.

"'Way to go, James. Affirmative action saves the day again.'

"I was really pained by that response, because I never even mentioned that I was African American on my college application, and yet people automatically assumed that was the only way a black guy could get into an Ivy League school."

While we understand James's dismay, we would encourage any college applicant to use every advantage to get in. The idea of wanting to be accepted on the basis of "pure" merit is all well and good, but there are many other factors that enter into the equation.

For example, the child of a university alumnus has a far better chance of gaining admission than the average applicant—especially if that parent contributes heavily to the institution. Do you think most applicants in that position would not mention that their parents are alumni or contriubtors?

Racially smart people use race whenever it gives them a competitive advantage. If being African American will help you get into the college of your choice, why would you want to hide that fact—when others who are vying for your spot are doing everything possible to unseat you? Likewise, if you suspect that your race may be a hindrance, it would be unwise to mention it on your application.

Consider the fact that Chinese American students in San Francisco were denied entrance to one of that city's top public high schools solely on the basis of race. Chinese and other Asian Americans were producing such high scores on the entrance exam that students of other races were having a hard time competing. In 1999, the school district was forced to abandon this anti-Asian racial quota, which had lasted for sixteen years.[20]

In the current racial climate, nobody can be certain whether any given race or ethnicity will provide an edge—whether you're seeking university admission or a corporate promotion. Still, this much is clear: Whenever you can use race to your advantage, don't hesitate. Do the smart thing, and seize the opportunity.

EIGHT

THE BUSINESS OF
EVERYDAY LIFE

Success is to be measured not so much by the position that one has achieved in life as by the obstacles which one has overcome while trying to succeed.

—BOOKER T. WASHINGTON[1]

The domain of everyday life encompasses all your dealings as a consumer, situations in which you pay money to get goods or services—such as shopping in stores, eating in restaurants, taking taxis, and transacting business in banks and airports. In a broader sense, this domain also comprises casual and social interactions that occur outside the workplace—but which often have some relation to business.

In most everyday exchanges, there is something you want from the person with whom you are negotiating. Your goal may be prompt and courteous service, or simply avoiding negative interactions. To the extent that your everyday dealings are diversity encounters, effective racial communication comes into play. And as always, your negotiating skills determine how successful you'll be in getting what you want.

NEGOTIATING IN A MULTIFACETED DOMAIN

There are several useful ways to look at the business of everyday life. From the perspective of your dealings as a consumer, it's the flipside of customer service. Here, you are the customer rather than the salesperson. As a consumer, you have a number of legal protections.

A taxi driver, for example, is not allowed to pass up an individual on the basis of race, just as a landlord cannot refuse to rent an apartment because of race. In reality, cab drivers in many cities regularly bypass African Americans—even celebrities. Similarly, non-white people are often turned down by landlords and sellers when they attempt to rent or purchase a house. It's often difficult to prove this kind of discrimination in court. However, if it can be documented or verified, the offending party may suffer a great deal of embarrassment and serious legal consequences.

The guidelines for smart racial communication in everyday life are similar to those for dealing with the system, even when the outcome isn't likely to have legal ramifications. On the surface, there may not appear to be very much at stake in your routine negotiations with waiters, taxi drivers, airline personnel, or bank clerks. Still, don't ever underestimate the power of those who appear to be in low-level service positions. Consider the following scenarios:

- You're trying to buy an airline ticket, but what if the ticket clerk decides to misplace your reservations?
- You've entered a taxi, but what if the driver decides to take the long route—or deliver you to the wrong destination?
- You've ordered lunch for you and a client, but what if the waitress gets hostile and takes forever to bring your food?

These are not hypothetical situations. They are everyday occurrences that often result from unsuccessful negotiations. Keep in mind that each of these everyday dealings is a workplace situation from the perspective of the individual being paid to do that job. In theory, that should be motivation enough to provide you with good service. But since life takes place in the real world, it's never wise to assume the other person is going to act rationally.

Always be prepared to take the lead in pursuing your objectives. When it comes to realizing your goals as a customer, racially smart interactions can save time, money, and aggravation. In addition, you can use your experiences negotiating these everyday dealings to monitor your personal strengths and insecurities in other business communications.

Sales professionals and entrepreneurs are often advised to view all their activities as a part of business. That may be stretching the point a bit. Nevertheless, racially unsmart behavior in a seemingly casual context can have business ramifications.

For example, the person you are rude to on a train or elevator may turn out be a customer whose business you covet. Or the customer may be a passerby who happens to observe your inappropriate behavior with someone else. These scenarios may strike you as unlikely, but they come up more often than you might imagine.

Although different circumstances evoke particular types of diversity encounters, racial intelligence is a portable set of skills that facilitate all your dealings. Once these skills become part of your operational style, they get hardwired into all your business and social encounters. So, if you can communicate effectively with people you encounter going to work, in airports, and in restaurants, you're likely to relate skillfully in business and other critical circumstances.

Diversity encounters that take place in the course of everyday exchanges may sometimes appear to have no specific business- or career-related ramifications. They tend to have a more casual feel, so you may be less alert than you'd normally be in encounters with business associates or authority figures who appear to have more power over your life. Still, trouble has a nasty way of striking at times when your guard is down.

WHITE FEAR VERSUS BLACK ANGER

"Oh my God, there's a nigger at my door," one of our survey respondents recalls hearing an elderly white woman caller beseeching a white radio talk show host while she was driving outside Los Angeles during the early 1960s.

"Don't worry, darlin'," the white host said reassuringly. "I'll alert the police right away."

It turned out that the black man had noticed that the woman had forgotten to turn off her car headlights, and was simply trying to extend a courtesy.

Race relations have come a long way since those days, yet one has to wonder just how much the emotions that provoked that fearful phone call have truly receded.

True, there are statistics indicating that African American males are far more likely to be arrested and convicted for violent crimes than their white counterparts. And while such statistics are often quoted to support a particular political agenda, these feelings are pervasive in our culture—and not just among white people.

"There is nothing more painful for me," civil rights leader Jesse Jackson is quoted as saying, "than to walk down the street and hear footsteps and start thinking about robbery—and then look around and see somebody white and feel relieved."[2]

Jackson later claimed that his remarks were taken out of context. However, they are frequently trotted out as a justification for racial profiling. If Jesse Jackson is afraid of his own kind, the reasoning goes, how are white folks supposed to feel?

In reality, the chances of a given white person being the victim of a criminal act by a black person is far too small to justify the level of terror everyday contacts can provoke. Nevertheless, the consequences of such fear, and the resulting anger it arouses on the part of some blacks, is a key factor in many everyday diversity encounters.

Worry about crime is cited as the primary reason cab drivers won't pick up black passengers in some urban areas. Similar fears drive store owners and managers to suspect black customers of being potential thieves. Casual contacts between blacks and whites can result in similar behaviors, and sometimes provoke complicated, and even extreme, emotional responses.

Craig, a white journalist, recalled a diversity encounter he had when he was a graduate fellow at a university in New York City:

"Certain floors of the journalism building were locked to protect the valuable equipment there. You needed a special key to enter, though students sometimes held the door open for people they recognized.

"One night, as I was entering one of these restricted floors, I saw a tall black man carrying an aluminum attaché case directly behind me. He grabbed hold of the door and entered before I could shut it. I had never seen this guy before, and I felt that it was my responsibility to make sure he was authorized to enter that area. So, I asked to see his ID.

"My request seemed to make him very angry, and he said something to the effect of: 'The only reason you're asking me for identification is because I'm black.' At that point, he shoved some sort of ID in my face. I was too flustered and upset to read the ID card, because I felt this person was unfairly and aggressively calling me a racist. In my mind, I was just trying to do the responsible thing. It would have been much easier to ignore him and keep going."

Was this a case of black anger reacting to white fear? Craig wasn't certain. In any case, our primary concern was to help this man reframe the scenario in terms of finding the most effective strategy for dealing with the situation.

"Would you have had the same reaction if the man was white?" we asked.

"I'm not sure," Craig answered. "I would hope that race didn't factor into the equation—though I certainly noticed that the man was black. For whatever reason, he didn't look like a journalism student. If he'd been white, and carrying a book bag, I'd like to think I'd have behaved the same way. However, I'm not sure."

The key for Craig was to learn about his own mind-set and that of the other person, and to use this knowledge in order to act more effectively in the future. Consider, for example, what the consequences of Craig's actions might be in a more traditional business context, if the black man he offended was a new client or an important executive.

While this uncomfortable encounter had no specific adverse consequences for Craig, the incident continued to provoke powerfully mixed feelings in him ten years later.

"If the same thing happened today," we asked, "is there anything you would do differently?"

"If I hadn't felt so on-the-spot, I might have gone to the security people in the building, and talked to them about the situation."

In Chapter Three, we discuss the need to develop a buffer zone between emotional reactions and the potential consequences of expressing them. As we note there, a personal buffer zone can help you isolate your feelings and process them before you act.

Here's how the process would work in the encounter Craig described:

- *Acknowledge your feelings.* Craig needed to face the fact that the man's race factored into his response, even if there were other considerations.
- *Evaluate the source of your feelings.* Craig admitted that, to some extent, he had acted on the stereotype that black men are more likely to commit crimes. In the heat of the moment, that predisposition held a great deal of sway over his response.
- *Choose the most effective way to address your concerns.* In retrospect, Craig recognized that there was a better way to negotiate the situation. Under the circumstances, going to security would have been a much smarter response than confronting the man directly and provoking a hostile encounter.

In Chapter Three, we discussed the importance of learning from every experience, and making effective use of this knowledge in future encounters. Fortunately for Craig, the only real consequence of acting on his emotions was some discomfort at the time and the lingering doubts about his motivation. Nevertheless, he appears to have given some thought to his behavior and profited from the experience.

African Americans who are confronted by stereotypical fear on the part of whites sometimes let their anger vent itself in irrational ways. An incident that the African American author Brent Staples recounts in his book *Parallel Time* captures this dynamic.

When Staples was a young graduate student at the University of Chicago, he liked to walk a particular route to his apartment. He always tried to act pleasant and friendly to the people he passed, but it didn't take long for him to notice that white people were going out of their way to avoid him. Although hurting anyone was the furthest thing from his mind, he watched as white people went through all sorts of machinations to sidestep him when he approached.

As his frustration turned to anger, Staples decided to strike back. Since people had prejudged him as threatening, he would fulfill their nightmare fantasies by intentionally doing things to scare them. The following excerpts come from Brent Staples's description of how he vented his anger:

"I'd been walking the street grinning good evening at people who were frightened to death of me. I did violence to them by just being. . . . Couples locked arms or reached for each other's hand when they saw me. Some crossed to the other side of the street. People who were carrying on conversations went mute and stared straight ahead, as though avoiding my eyes would save them. . . .

"I began to avoid people. I turned out of my way into side streets to spare them the sense that they were being stalked. I let them clear the lobbies of the buildings before I entered, so they wouldn't feel trapped. . . . Then I changed. . . .

"One night I stooped beneath the branches and came up on the other side, just as a couple was stepping from their car into their town house. The woman pulled her purse close with one hand and reached for her husband with the other. The two of them stood frozen as I bore down on them. I felt a surge of power: these people were mine; I could do with them as I wished. If I'd been younger with less to lose, I'd have robbed them, and it would have been easy. All I'd have to do was stand silently before them until they surrendered their money. [Instead,] I thundered, 'Good evening' into their bleached-out faces and cruised away laughing.

"I held a special contempt for people who cowered in their cars as they waited for the light to change. . . . They hammered the door locks when I came into view. Once I had hustled down the street, head down, trying to seem harmless. Now I turned brazenly into the headlights and laughed. They'd made me terrifying. Now I'd show them how terrifying I could be."[3]

UNDERSTANDING PING-PONGING STEREOTYPES

It is highly doubtful that Brent Staples, now in his fifties, would engage in such risky behavior today. Still, the emotions that drove him are understandable—even if the resulting behavior was anything but smart.

When you are conducting yourself in a civilized, even friendly, manner, people responding to you as if you're a criminal is a hostile and hurtful communication—as well as an assault to your ego. Which raises another critical step in the racial intelligence process.

• Know what you want to accomplish. Define your personal objective in each encounter. Always think before you react. Ask yourself: What do I want to get out of this interaction? Once you recognize what matters most in the situation, try to stay with that goal. Don't allow yourself to become sidetracked by superfluous issues, ego trips, or emotions.

The feelings Brent Staples describe emanate from the essence of one's being, and touch the core of a person's self-esteem. However, to avoid getting trapped, the racially smart man or woman tempers these emotions by engaging in the following rational thought process:

1. *Question the other person's behavior.* Ask yourself, what is making this person afraid? Is it a response to me as an individual, or is it a reaction to a stereotype I happen to fit?

2. *Recognize that reacting in kind to another person's racial ignorance never serves your purpose, unless your aim is to provoke that individual.* You have a very limited amount of control over someone

else's reaction to your race. You may able to manipulate that individual's response to some extent through things like body language and dress. However, if someone has decided in advance that all members of a certain race pose a threat, you have virtually no influence over how that person will act when he or she first meets you. On the other hand, you do have a great deal to say in terms of the situation's ultimate outcome, but this depends on how you counteract the initial hostility.

When someone confronts you with a negative stereotype, he or she is effectively challenging you to a game of racial ping-pong. The first volley begins with the fearful person's stereotype. The question then becomes, how do you react when the ball lands on your side of the table?

Do you recognize the biased reaction as essentially the other person's problem, or do you allow it to rule your emotions?

The kind of angry response Brent Staples exhibited presents a challenge. The ball is now back on the other person's side of the table. Does he recoil in fear or run away? If so, getting even may provide a moment of bittersweet satisfaction for the individual unjustly targeted by another's racial fear. Still, that kind of response also carries certain dangers.

What if the other person panics and pulls a gun on you? Or, what if a police car suddenly appears, and the fearful person decides to report your threatening actions. Do you challenge the officer's authority, or tell him that you were only joking? Either way, you have volleyed yourself into a corner. Chances are that your evening will turn out a lot grimmer than you had planned.

3. Keep your objective in sight—without sacrificing your self-respect. Under circumstances like those Brent Staples described, the goal is not very ambitious: to take a walk in peace, and to be treated with common courtesy. However, when someone responds to you with unfounded fear, another goal comes to the fore: staying out of trouble.

Remember, you are not obligated to make someone who confronts you with a racial stereotype feel more comfortable. Ignoring people like that may be the smartest response. You have a life to lead, and business to conduct. Why let someone else's ignorance trap you into playing racial ping-pong? This is one game that has no winners.

GUIDELINES FOR AVOIDING ESCALATING STEREOTYPES

If you genuinely fear people of another racial group, question the basis of those fears. Many people who harbor stereotypes have never had a bad (or any) interaction with someone of the feared race.

Ignorance is the mother of fear. Listening to all the political rhetoric about race on radio talk shows or watching crime reports on television can make people afraid, especially when those canned stereotypes can't be counteracted by actual experience. However, there are many rewards to approaching a diversity encounter with an open mind instead of fear. Nan, a business librarian from Arizona, found this out shortly after she relocated to New York City.

"I was walking on the Upper West Side on Saint Patrick's Day. I'd only been living in New York for a few months, and I had hardly any experience interacting with black people. Suddenly, I noticed a young black man walking toward me. He didn't appear to be threatening. Still, I'd been warned about the dangers for single women on the streets of Manhattan.

"I felt somewhat frightened, and thought about crossing the street to avoid coming face-to-face with the black man. But, at the last second, I decided to take a chance. My heart started beating faster as the man approached. Then, suddenly, he tipped his hat and said in an Irish brogue, 'Top of the mornin', lassie.'

"I took this experience as a good omen about New York City, and a lesson in not being too quick to prejudge people on the basis of racial stereotypes."

In general, we endorse Nan's approach. It's irrational to use race as the basis for fear. On the other hand, we would not ask anyone to ignore any gut feeling of danger. If your mind and body tell you that you're in danger, you should take immediate steps to get out of the situation. It's dumb to stick around for the sake of political correctness, or to prove that you're not bigoted. However, once you're out of harm's way, ask yourself the following questions:

- Was race the only basis for your fear?
- If not, what other signals were you picking up?
- If your fear was based solely on race, what experiences or impressions formed the foundation of your feeling?
- Given the same set of circumstances, would you respond in the same way?

As Gavin De Becker, security consultant and author of *The Gift of Fear,* has observed:

"True fear is a survival signal that sounds in the presence of danger . . . [and] protects us, but unwarranted fear has assumed a power over us that it holds over no other creature on Earth."[4]

De Becker cites statistics showing that most murders are committed by individuals who are well known to the victim. Still, people seem to be more afraid of random violence by strangers. Perhaps fear of the unknown is why people tend to be more scared and distrustful of those who are racially different. This response may be understandable, but it is neither smart or adaptive.

When people interpret one's race as the primary signal of danger, they can overlook behaviors that truly are threatening—and that have nothing to do with skin color.

WHAT DO PEOPLE FEAR MOST?[5]

A poll of 1,009 adults reported in *USA Today* revealed the things that Americans fear most. The following are some of the events of which respondents said they were "afraid" or "very afraid":

1.	54 percent	Being in a car crash
2.	53 percent	Contracting cancer
3.	49 percent	Lacking money for retirement
4.	36 percent	Food poisoning from meat
5.	35 percent	Getting Alzheimer's disease
6.	33 percent	Being a victim of violence
7.	28 percent	Contracting AIDS

8.	25 percent	Natural disasters
9.	22 percent	Being killed in a plane crash
10.	18 percent	Being a victim of mass violence
11.	16 percent	Being audited by the IRS
12.	15 percent	Being accused of sexual harassment
13.	11 percent	Being the victim of sexual harassment

Interestingly, the researchers found blacks to be more fearful than whites in all the above categories.

GOOD MANNERS, SOUND JUDGMENT, AND SMART RACIAL COMMUNICATION

In the course of your everyday negotiations, you are likely to encounter people of different racial and cultural backgrounds. The key to dealing with them effectively is not to ignore their race, but to act respectfully and courteously to everyone who crosses your path.

Certain courses of action are based as much on common sense as racial intelligence. For example, when you are interacting with restaurant servers, it's a given that you'll get further by treating them respectfully, instead of reminding them that their sole purpose in life is to wait on you. If you're at a business lunch, your clients and colleagues are likely to judge you, in part, by the way you treat others. If, for example, you snap at a server who happens to be black, others in your party may label you as biased.

Whether it's a bank teller, a store clerk, or the maintenance person who empties the office trash, everyone likes to feel valued and appreciated. You will always receive better service if you treat people courteously. This strategy can be especially effective in diversity encounters, because respectful treatment goes a long way in defusing other people's negative expectations.

It's useful for white people to understand that African Americans are prone to experience certain kinds of slights quite frequently, and are likely to respond positively when those expectations are not confirmed. For example, black people frequently complain that whites push ahead of them on store lines and generally disrespect them. Consequently, they are likely to be especially appreciative when whites go out of their way to show respect.

Another common complaint among blacks is that whites often don't respond appropriately to their position or professional status. Many African Americans we interviewed are sensitive to being addressed by their first names by white people they don't know well. Likewise, an African American Ph.D. may be more sensitive than her white counterpart to being called by her first name (or even as "Ms.") instead of "Doctor."

This sensitivity may be rooted in what some African Americans perceive to be techniques whites have used historically to assert their superiority over the "darker races," such as addressing them with condescension or contempt.

Remember, every human encounter is mediated by the respect people demonstrate toward one another. It's important to monitor and recognize any stereotypes you may be harboring, so that they don't pop up at the wrong time and offend someone who may be important to you.

Many problematic encounters in everyday dealings are the result of poor judgment and bad manners. When a dose of racial ignorance is added to the mix, you've got a toxic combination.

We interviewed a number of African Americans who complained about being followed, ignored, or given second-rate treatment by store salesmen. The smart response to such treatment is to take your business elsewhere, which amounts to an instant economic boycott. Considering what's at stake, it's puzzling that any salesperson would display such self-defeating behavior.

Could the stereotype of a poor, uneducated black be so ingrained that it's not worth a few minutes of the salesman's time to approach the individual as a customer, and develop a customer profile based on relevant economic facts?

A racially smart company needs to train all its employees—particularly those who come in contact with the public—to deal with any kind of customer. As a consumer, you can provide companies and salespeople with the motivation to become more responsive by exercising your economic power.

"I may not be able to change the world," Alex, a forty-three-year-old African American dentist, remarked. "However, I can spend my money in places where I'm treated with dignity.

"When I was younger, I used to get angry when salesmen gave me shoddy treatment," Alex continued. "A few times, I even made a scene. I eventually realized that it's not worth getting my blood pressure up because of other people's prejudice. My money is just as green as the next guy's. If a salesperson is too stupid to realize that, it's his loss—not mine."

STRATEGIES FOR DEALING WITH EVERYDAY SLIGHTS

Blacks and other minorities suffer a variety of indignities in negotiating everyday commerce that most whites never experience. Here are some suggestions for avoiding or countering them:

Taxi Drivers Who Won't Pick You Up

In New York City, cab drivers welcome properly dressed white men into their back seats. However, African American males (and black women too) are likely to find that clothes don't make much difference. Several cabbies told us that new drivers are counseled by veterans not to pick up any black people, if at all possible. "Even the good ones can take you into a ghetto neighborhood," one driver told us. "Then, when they get out, some crackhead jumps into the back seat and holds you up."

You can write down the license numbers of taxis that pass you by, and report the drivers to the appropriate authorities. Still, that's not much consolation to a black person who's standing out in the rain while cabs pass him by to pick up white passengers.

One African American businessman who frequently takes taxis in Manhattan sometimes stands next to someone who is white, or asks that person to hail a cab on his behalf.

"Some white people are sympathetic to the problems blacks have getting taxi drivers to stop—and will agree to play along," he told us. "Others have offered to share a cab."

Another possibility is setting up an account with a reliable car service. In many areas, these services don't cost more than taxis, and a phone call will bring a car and driver to your location. This is a particularly useful approach when you are with clients or business associates. At times like this, you don't want to let the anger and frustration of not getting a taxi pose a negative distraction.

Restaurants that Don't Value Your Patronage

Service in restaurants can reflect the views of ownership, or on-site management, or the wait staff. Everyone experiences poor service from time to time, and that's never pleasant. But the feeling that the lousy service is racially motivated can be especially hard to digest. Restaurant service is supposed to be color-blind—as both a matter of law and good business. But here is another instance where bias and bad judgment sometimes override good business sense.

Lawrence Otis Graham is a Harvard-educated corporate lawyer and author who conducted a survey of ten top New York restaurants. Noting that he usually receives acceptable treatment when he dines with white friends or clients, Graham made it a point to eat with other black professionals or his African American wife.

According to Graham, he was handed coats in half of the restaurants while waiting to be seated, as if he were the coat-check person. In seven of the ten restaurants, he was offered tables closest to the kitchen or the bathroom—even when more desirable seating was available.

"While any one of these incidents could be dismissed as a result of innocent carelessness, [the] cumulative effect in a black person's daily existence is disturbing," Graham comments in his book, *Member of the Club*.

"I almost always avoid restaurants with valet parking because of the times I've been handed keys by incoming white patrons who assume that I am there to park cars. . . .

"Whether it's because of the racial attitudes of the wait staff, the maitre d', or the patrons, randomly selecting one of New York's better restaurants for a business meal, a first date, or a family celebration is a tremendous risk for even the most forgiving black person. . . . I found [that] . . . food quality and ambience can take a backseat to common courtesy when it comes to being black and trying to dine with the same dignity that is accorded to white patrons."[6]

We have heard these complaints from other black professionals, though a few claim to have experienced no problem taking clients and friends to some of the same places. Nonwhites are increasingly able to dine out with the reasonable expectation that they will be treated courteously. In any case, it's usually best to assume good-will, while not ignoring the possibility of encountering bias.

If you are dining out with a new or particularly important client, consider going only to places in which you've had positive experiences. If you receive poor treatment in an unfamiliar establishment and your guest shares this discomfort, try to make a graceful exit— but not before discreetly informing the restaurant manager why you are leaving.

There may be other instances where the discrimination is more subtle, or your guest doesn't pick up on it. In that case, consider your primary objective in the situation.

If you're trying to close a sale or impress a colleague, it may be best not to make a scene. If, however, your guest becomes aware of the problem and wants to leave, by all means do so. Again, file your complaint with the manager of the establishment, and let that person know that you intend to share your bad experience with others. Remind this individual that sensitive people of all colors are likely to avoid businesses that treat customers of any race shabbily.

Security Personnel Who Practice Racial Profiling

In Chapter Three, we discuss the issue of racial profiling by store security people, from the perspective of both the profiler and the individual being targeted. Please see that section for detailed advice on how to negotiate such encounters successfully.

Recently, there has been an increase of reported incidents of racial profiling by airport security officials. This can be especially troubling for men and women who travel frequently on business.

Searches of person and property can cause delays and stress that can impede your ability to conduct business effectively. Sometimes the results are traumatic. Consider what happened at the Raleigh-Durham, North Carolina, airport to former Virginia governor Douglas Wilder, an African American, while he was en route home from a business trip.

"When I went through the airport metal detector check, the buzzer sounded," Governor Wilder recalls. "After taking everything out of my pockets, I went through the check for the second time when it dawned on me that it could have been my suspenders [that set off the buzzer].

"When I told the white security man that it must be my suspenders, he literally snapped. He grabbed me, then pushed me and choked me. It was like an out-of-body experience. I just couldn't believe what was happening to me."[7]

Wilder, who eventually settled a $5 million lawsuit against the airport, the airport security service, and the security guard, commented, "A human being shouldn't be treated this way, no matter what his position or color."

The circumstances Governor Wilder encountered at the airport are essentially the same as dealing with police officers. When you are confronted by people in authority, particularly those who are carrying guns, the smartest strategy is to be cooperative and nonconfrontational, in hopes of ending the encounter as soon as humanly possible. Save your formal complaint for a later time. (For specific information on how best to accomplish this, please see Chapter Seven.)

We have examined in great depth the phenomenon of racial profiling, and to us it makes no sense. Businesses have every right to develop profiles of potentially troublesome individuals. However, research shows that nonracial factors such as body language, signs of intoxication, or a past criminal record are far better predictors of dangerous behavior. Yet, a person's color continues to be the profiling criterion security personnel and their employers prefer. But why?

The most likely answer is that it takes no training or intelligence to discriminate in this way. After all, what could be easier than evaluating people strictly on the basis of lighter or darker skin? To recognize the real potential thieves and ferret them out would require a certain amount of information, discretion, and forethought.

As long as businesses and public agencies continue to use this facile but costly approach to determine whom to frisk in airports and whom to scrutinize in department stores, they will continue to waste resources covering their tracks and fighting lawsuits and negative publicity.

NINE

WHAT THE RQ TEST
TELLS YOU

We are the people our parents warned us about.
— JIMMY BUFFETT (AUTHOR/SINGER-SONGWRITER)

CALCULATING YOUR RQ

Now that you've had an opportunity to explore smart strategies for negotiating a variety of diversity encounters, you are ready to compare your responses to the RQ questions in Chapter Two to the strategies you might employ to handle similar scenarios, when they come up in the future. To calculate your numerical RQ, please score each question as follows:

Each lettered choice is rated with a score of 5, 4, 3, 2, or 1. Select the score that matches your response. Then total your scores for each of the twenty questions. *Five* (5) is the most racially intelligent response; *one* (1) is the least racially intelligent response. Please note that several questions do not offer all five choices.

- A score of 85 to 100 suggests a high degree of racial intelligence.
- A score of 70 to 84 suggests a moderate degree of racial intelligence.
- A score below 70 suggests that there are gaps in racial intelligence.

QUESTION NUMBER	ANSWER LETTER					YOUR ANSWER (Please fill in answers from Chapter 2)	YOUR SCORE
	a	b	c	d	e		
1	a=3	b=1	c=2	d=3	e=5	d	3
2	a=1	b=3	c=2	d=1	e=5	e	5
3	a=2	b=1	c=1	d=4	e=5	a	2
4	a=3	b=2	c=1	d=1	e=5	b	2
5	a=5	b=3	c=1	d=2	e=3	a	5
6	a=1	b=3	c=1	d=2	e=5	e	5
7	a=1	b=4	c=2	d=3	e=5	e	5
8	a=1	b=2	c=1	d=5	e=2	c	1
9	a=5	b=1	c=2	d=3	e=1	e	1
10	a=3	b=5	c=2	d=1	e=2	b	5
11	a=2	b=1	c=1	d=1	e=5	e	5
12	a=2	b=2	c=1	d=5	e=1	d	5
13	a=2	b=5	c=3	d=1	e=4	e	4
14	a=1	b=3	c=2	d=1	e=5	e	5
15	a=5	b=1	c=2	d=1	e=1	a	5
16	a=5	b=1	c=3	d=1	e=2	d	1
17	a=3	b=1	c=5	d=1	e=1	c	5
18	a=5	b=1	c=1	d=1	e=5	a	5
19	a=5	b=2	c=1	d=3	e=3	b	2
20	a=5	b=2	c=3	d=1	e=1	a	5
Please add the numbers in the boxes for your TOTAL SCORE:							76

EVALUATING YOUR RESPONSES

Now that you have calculated your numerical RQ score, we're going to talk about why certain choices make more sense than others. It is quite possible that you will disagree with some of our conclusions, and that's okay. The most important thing is that you put yourself in the place of the main character in each of the scenarios, and use the concepts we've explored throughout the book to project the likely impact of each choice.

1. Domain: The Workplace

You are a <u>*white supervisor*</u> *in a corporation that has had complaints of racism in the past. A group of four black secretaries asks to speak to you about their perception of a hostile workplace atmosphere.*

What is your first response?

a. "I cannot talk to you until I call the company lawyer." (3)
This response is overly defensive. It immediately announces your inability to resolve the problem, as well as your lack of concern.

b. "Tell me what you people want." (1)
A highly offensive response. Certain expressions have cultural connotations that go beyond their literal meanings. When a white person refers to blacks as "you people," he may effectively be perceived as having used the "N word."

c. "This company has a nondiscrimination policy that we adhere to strictly." (2)
This is tantamount to either an admission that a problem exists or a statement of complete indifference. These women have a right to expect their supervisor to listen to their concerns. Responding with legal gibberish is the same as saying, "I just don't care."

d. "Tell me what is causing you concern." (3)

This may well be the most sensitive response, but it ignores some important realities about contemporary diversity issues. Please see the comment keyed to choice *e* below for why this well-meaning approach can backfire.

e. "Please put your concerns in writing." (5)

This is clearly the right way to go in a corporate environment— particularly since you are talking to four people, each of whom may have a different perception of the problem. With time, verbal interchanges become subject to people's faulty recollections. When the complaints are written down, there can be no dispute about what was said at the meeting.

2. Domain: The Workplace

You are a <u>black sales associate</u> in an upscale department store. You sense that white customers often avoid you and gravitate toward the white sales associates. This is a problem for you because the salespeople in this store work on commission.

How do you handle the situation?

a. Get angry and tell the white customers that you can take care of them as well as a white salesperson can. (1)

This is an extremely poor choice for anyone in a sales position. Your job is to serve the customer. Any negative feelings need to be dealt with at another time.

b. Quit and look for a job in a store with more black customers, because you can never be successful in this environment. (3)

This may be necessary as a long-term strategy, but that's something to consider when you are away from the immediate situation. One important question to ask yourself in making this decision would be: Is the clientele in this store especially racist, or have I decided that dealing with white customers is just too much of an uphill battle?

   c. Ask your white coworker to steer some of her customers your way. (2)
This is unlikely to work, considering that you and the white salesperson are competing for commissions. However, there may be favors you can do for the coworker (like covering shifts) that would motivate her to help you out. Also, be aware that making such a request might be interpreted as an appeal for affirmative action—a questionable strategy in this context.

   d. Do nothing to alter the situation. (1)
Taking a passive approach to a situation that threatens your livelihood is never a good idea—regardless of whether race is a factor. Such indifference is particularly counterproductive for sales professionals.

   e. Go out of your way to approach the white customers and help them look past their racial biases. (5)
This is the best strategy by far. To be successful in sales, you must learn how to deal with all kinds of people. It's natural for some customers to gravitate to a salesperson of their own race, but this doesn't make them racists. You have to rely on your strengths. Perhaps you are more personable or competent than your coworker. Maybe you have a more engaging smile. A proactive approach can quickly communicate any of these advantages, and cause more customers to seek you out.

3. Domain: Everyday Commerce

You are a well-dressed <u>black businessman</u> riding alone in an elevator. The door opens, and a middle-aged white woman enters. The woman moves as far away from you as possible. She is clearly afraid.

How do you react?

    a. Try to engage the woman in small talk. (2)

This is a chance meeting—brief and anonymous in nature. It has very little significance to either of you—except that she is frightened and you are aware of her response. There is no practical reason to engage this woman in conversation. This approach probably won't make either of you feel better. It may wind up making you both even more uncomfortable.

    b. Tell her that, even though you're black, she has no reason to be afraid. (1)

This response acknowledges that you understand the woman's discomfort, but doesn't serve to further anyone's interests. These words can come across as sarcastic—and this is something you might understandably want to convey. But sarcasm does neither of you any good. An attempt to utter these words with sincerity might give the impression that you are trying to take responsibility for a complete stranger's racial stereotypes—as well as your own. How would that serve your purpose?

    c. Since the woman has already prejudged you as dangerous, move closer to her and flash a sinister smile. (1)

This response is understandable for someone who is repeatedly and wrongly stereotyped as dangerous. A part of you may well want to say, "Since you find me so terrifying, I'll give you a reason to be scared." However, reacting in this angry manner may result in the woman calling the police or security personnel. She might even spray you with mace. This would serve to make a bad situation far worse.

    d. Give the woman a friendly nod, take a step away, and pretend she's not even there. (4)

This is the second-smartest course of action. You are using body language to acknowledge the woman's feelings, while attempting to assume a physically nonthreatening posture. Still, do you really feel like being friendly to someone who has prejudged you in this way?

e. Suppress your feelings. Do and say nothing. (5)

A black person may come to expect some whites to fear him, but he can never truly accept being the target of bias. Why, in this brief encounter, should you be the least bit cordial to somebody who has made an assumption based on negative racial stereotypes? You have nothing to gain by making this person feel more comfortable. A spurned attempt to do so might make you feel even more demeaned.

4. Domain: Everyday Commerce

You are a white woman on an elevator that was full of people when you first got on. Suddenly, you notice that everyone has gotten off—except you and a young black man. You feel uncomfortable.

How do you react?

a. Suppress your feelings. Do and say nothing. (3)

This may be a sensible response, depending on the intensity of your fears. Unless you sense genuine danger signals, not just the man's black skin, the chances of coming to harm are small.

b. Start talking about the weather, and hope his friendly response will put your mind at ease. (2)

You can try this approach, and see if the man's response eases or intensifies your fears. But if this person means you harm, he's not likely to be moved by this ploy. If he had no interest in you before, he will either be friendly or ignore you.

c. Put your hand in your purse so he'll think you're carrying a weapon. (1)

This is a poor strategy. It's possible that someone who means you harm will be deterred, but this ploy can also turn a neutral situation into one fraught with danger. The young man might believe you mean to harm him and take defensive action.

d. Strike up a conversation. Tell the man that you're all in favor of affirmative action. (1)

This disingenuous approach only serves to communicate a negative feeling toward black people. It won't provoke a physical attack, but you may be in for some well-deserved harsh words.

e. Get off at the next floor and wait for another elevator. (5)

This is the wisest course of action whenever you feel vulnerable or threatened. If your fears are a result of negative racial stereotypes, you can deal with those feelings later. This elevator is not the right place to prove that you are free of racial bias. Your safety should always be more important than the need to appear politically correct.

5. Domain: The System

You are a <u>white parent</u> taking your sick child to a pediatrician assigned by your new health maintenance organization (HMO). You walk into the examination room to find that the doctor is black. You have no experience with African American doctors, and you're not especially comfortable with the prospect.

What do you do?

a. Be pleasant and don't respond to the doctor's color. Allow him to examine your child. Who knows? You may like this doctor. (5)

This is clearly the most effective choice. A person's race tells you nothing about his or her level of skill. Once you go through an initial visit, you can evaluate the doctor using criteria that are far more relevant than race.

b. Find some pretense to leave. Walk out of the office. Inform your HMO that you will only accept a white doctor. (3)

This is smarter than c or d, even if it amounts to a confession of racial bias. Nevertheless, you are entitled to be treated by a physician with whom you feel comfortable. If the doctor's race is that much of an issue for you, it is your right to refuse.

c. Congratulate the doctor for getting so far in life. Tell him that he sets a good example for other blacks to follow. (1)

This is the least smart choice. It communicates that you buy into racial stereotypes, and strongly hints there are things you aren't saying that are even more biased.

d. Tell the doctor nobody in your immediate family has ever had a black physician before. Admit that you feel a little nervous about his examining your child. (2)

This response is marginally better than c, only because it is more an expression of genuine feelings, rather than a rote recitation of stereotypes. Nevertheless, this is an ill-advised communication. Under these circumstances, you gain nothing by bringing up the issue of race.

e. Walk out without offering an explanation. (3)

As is the case with response b, you have a right to request a doctor with whom you feel comfortable. Arguably, it is a more palatable response than b, because it calls less attention to what you are doing. However, both responses would be totally senseless if your child required immediate medical attention.

6. Domain: The Workplace

You are a <u>white administrator</u> who feels uncomfortable because one of your colleagues regularly tells racist jokes when no blacks or Hispanics are around.

The best way to handle this situation is to:

a. Laugh at the jokes. (1)

This is an inappropriate and unintelligent response in a workplace setting. It can make you as culpable as the colleague who is telling the biased jokes.

b. Immediately tell your supervisor. (3)

You may eventually have to take this step, but it's usually more advisable to talk with the colleague first. However, if the troublesome language continues, you should report it to the appropriate individual.

c. Do nothing. (1)

This is an ill-advised strategy, one that others in the company can interpret as tacitly supporting a discriminatory environment.

d. Contact a lawyer. (2)

This is an overreaction. It does nothing to address the problem or to further your interests.

e. Take the colleague aside and talk to him. (5)

This is, by far, the best course of action. It gives the colleague a chance to reflect on what he's doing, and lays the groundwork for further action on your part, should that become necessary.

7. Domain: The System

You are a <u>black high school senior</u> applying for admission to college.

Which is your best strategy?

a. Send a letter with the application telling them you are black. (1)

This is too blatant a playing of the race card—something you should not do unless you are certain it will further your objectives. Also, some admissions officers might think you have a chip on your shoulder.

b. List black-identified groups under extracurricular activities or mention them in your essay. (4)

Indicating that you are African American in the context of creating a bigger picture of your experience isn't likely to hurt your chances. However, it would be more useful to find out beforehand if mentioning race is likely to be helpful.

c. Ask to see the school's written affirmative action policy. (2)

This comes off as a strident request, especially since virtually every college has some kind of affirmative action or diversity policy.

d. Make no reference to race. (3)

Some minority candidates want to be judged strictly on their academic merits so they can't be accused of having reaped an advantage based on affirmative action. These feelings are understandable, though some people will automatically assume that virtually all blacks who get into good colleges have benefited by affirmative action.

e. Find out all you can about the school. If you think it will be to your benefit, mention groups and activities that make your racial identification clear. (5)

It's always smart to use race—if it gives you a competitive advantage. However, to make an informed judgment, it's important that you research the situation in advance.

8. Domain: The Workplace

You are a <u>white supervisor</u> who sees a black employee distributing anti-Semitic material on a street corner after working hours.

What do you do?

a. Call the police. (1)

This is a useless response, since the employee's actions are probably not illegal.

b. Fire the employee. (2)

It's natural to want to get rid of a biased individual, particularly one who needs to publicize his views. Nevertheless, several court decisions have reversed such firings. People have a right to express bigoted views—even to hand out racist literature, however offensive those actions may be to others.

c. Ignore the incident. (1)

This course of action can come back to haunt you later. If, for example, the employee began acting out his biases on company premises, and it can be established that you had prior knowledge of these tendencies, you could be held accountable.

d. Notify human resources. (5)

This is your smartest course. Human resources needs to know about such an incident, so they can decide if it is necessary to monitor the employee's actions. Meanwhile, you have acted responsibly and minimized your exposure.

e. Confront the employee during working hours. (2)

This might be an appropriate response if the person was your peer. Even so, the individual's actions indicate overt racism, and he apparently has no compunction about displaying those views in public. In any case, since you are a supervisor and the incident did not occur on company grounds, you gain nothing by directly confronting the individual.

9. *Domain: The Workplace*

You are a <u>white professor</u> proctoring a final exam at a college that has had more than its share of racially sensitive issues in recent years. You spot a black student cheating on the test. The rules are clear: Any student caught cheating will be asked to leave the examination hall and given a failing grade on the test.

How do you handle the situation?

a. Immediately confront the student. Tell him you saw him cheating, and ask him to leave the room. (5)

This is the only principled—and racially intelligent—option, even if it is unpleasant. Any other approach would be unwise and unethical, and can lead to all sorts of complications.

b. Pretend you haven't noticed the cheating, so as not to provoke a confrontation, which could possibly leave you open to charges of racial bias. (1)

You may perceive this as a difficult situation, because the student is black. However, by closing your eyes to the cheating, you compromise the integrity of the institution, and put all the other students—white and black—at a disadvantage.

c. Quietly tell the student that, if you spot any more irregularities, you will have to ask him to leave. (2)

This course of action is only marginally better than the one in *b*. It can only be justified if you have no tangible proof that the student was cheating.

d. Call in a black colleague, and ask him to help you deal with the problem. (3)

This may be a last-ditch solution, if you truly fear creating a racial incident. However, calling in a black colleague under these circumstances is an ineffective way to deal with an issue that has nothing to do with race. In addition, there's a risk that you may offend the colleague.

e. Allow the student to complete the test, then call him aside and let him know that you saw him cheating. (1)

This response is quite possibly the worst of all. Aside from acting irresponsibly, you are announcing your inaction to the very person you are obliged to sanction.

10. Domain: The Workplace

You are a <u>white section supervisor</u> who overhears two black secretaries using the "N word" with each other.

What do you do?

a. Take no action. (3)

While it's well known that people of the same race sometimes use this kind of inside language with one another, these kinds of exchanges are inappropriate in a business setting. There is no way to be certain if some customer or service person will overhear the conversation and take offense. As a supervisor, you are responsible for the prevailing atmosphere. Nevertheless, a white person is on thin ice when he starts dictating language to blacks and other minorities. Therefore, if this is an isolated incident, saying nothing may be a strategy worth considering.

b. Politely tell the two secretaries that the "N word" is not to be used on company premises. (5)

This is the smartest course of action, even if you do have to step lightly in correcting these employees.

c. Tell the secretaries that you are offended by the "N word." (2)

This comes across as condescending and insincere. The issue isn't whether or not you're offended by the "N word." What you want to convey is that this kind of language has no place in a business environment.

d. Use the "N word" yourself in a humorous fashion. (1)

The most dangerous and least smart response. People who belong to the same racial group can say things to one another that are off-limits to outsiders. Furthermore, by using such language in the work-place, you become far more culpable than the two secretaries.

e. Threaten to report the secretaries to your superior. (2)

Bouncing something like this upstairs can exaggerate the serious-ness of what may well be a minor incident. It distances you from your employees, and demonstrates a lack of confidence and author-ity on your part.

11. Domain: The System

You are a <u>white motorist</u> driving a late-model car. Suddenly you are stopped on the freeway by a black policeman for going 64 mph *in a 55 mph zone. You've been driving this highway for years, and can't ever recall observing the speed limit. However, you always stay within the flow of traffic and have never received a speeding ticket.*

Under the circumstances, how do you react?

a. Point out to the cop that everyone else is going over the speed limit, and ask why he's making such a big deal out of nothing. (2)

This is a poor choice. You are technically in the wrong—and you need to acknowledge this to have any chance of driving away without a citation. It makes little difference that the officer didn't stop others who were going over the speed limit.

b. Ask the officer for his name and badge number. Tell him that this is clearly a case of discrimination. (1)

Accusing the officer of racism is even more ill-advised than the strategy in a. Playing the race card is never smart when you're holding such a weak hand.

c. Try to engage the officer in a friendly conversation about black athletes and entertainers. (1)

This response is no smarter than accusing the cop of bigotry. Bringing up your supposed affinity for black entertainers and athletes in this context is almost the same as saying, "Some of my best friends are black."

d. Offer the cop some cash if he'll let you go. (1)

This is a chancy strategy, one that can land you in far deeper trouble than a speeding ticket. Offering a bribe is particularly ill-advised in this context. A white person's assuming that a black officer would be willing to act dishonestly could easily be taken as a racial affront.

e. Apologize for going too fast, and ask the officer if he'd consider issuing a warning in lieu of a ticket. (5)

This is the smartest choice. In this instance, the best course is to act in a racially neutral fashion and to make no comment on the issue of race. This is not to say, however, that the situation is race-neutral. On the contrary, if you ignore the racial differences between you and the officer, you are more likely to say or do something that might create needless tension—and an unhappy outcome for you.

12. Domain: The Workplace

You are a <u>white middle manager</u> in a large corporation who has been having problems with your computer. Failure to resolve those problems may prevent you from meeting a critical deadline. The person in charge of authorizing computer repairs is a black woman, and you're convinced that she is purposely putting your repeated requests for help on the back burner.

How do you handle the situation?

a. Confront the woman, and ask why she refuses to help you with your problem. (2)
This approach is likely to get you nowhere. She may back down, but a head-on confrontation will probably make her more resistant.

b. File a written complaint with the woman's supervisor. (2)
This may be a last resort. However, complaining isn't likely to help your cause, unless you can produce some specific evidence that she's purposely trying to obstruct you. Also, most supervisors don't want to become involved in peer conflicts—especially when they have a gender or racial component.

c. Let yourself be overheard telling colleagues that the woman doesn't like you because you are a white man. (1)
The least smart response. You are effectively trying to play the race card in a game you can only lose. Far from making things better, you may be opening yourself up to charges of discrimination.

d. Approach the woman in private. Tell her that you know she is busy, but that you really would appreciate her help. Tell her that if the two of you can't resolve the situation, you will ask others in the department for help in solving your problem. (5)

Even though this is a diversity encounter, there is no way to know the extent to which race is a factor. Therefore, the smartest course of action in this case is to minimize the racial component, and to approach the colleague in a polite, sincere, and race-neutral manner.

e. Do and say nothing. Maybe the situation will somehow resolve itself. (1)

It's never smart to take a passive approach to problems. If you miss the deadline, nobody will be interested in your faulty computer. This situation requires focused, intelligent action.

13. Domain: The Workplace

You are a <u>black employee</u> who has been passed over for a promotion five times. On each of these occasions, you've asked your white supervisor for an explanation, but he has been evasive.

What do you do?

a. File a racial discrimination lawsuit. (2)

Taking legal action is an unwise first response, unless you've laid the groundwork in advance. Discrimination lawsuits are difficult, emotionally draining procedures—even if you can find an attorney to take one on a contingency basis. Instituting legal action is also likely to make your continuing tenure at that company far more uncomfortable.

b. Meet with your human resources representative. (5)

This is a smart response, because you are voicing your concerns within the company. You can then gauge whether those concerns are being addressed, and how to proceed from that point.

c. Start looking for another job. (3)

This may be a necessary strategy, if you conclude that you are not being rewarded based on your performance.

d. Do nothing. Accept that it's often hard for blacks to get ahead in Corporate America. (1)

This is a defeatist and demoralizing approach. Racial bias still exists in Corporate America, but making this an excuse for inaction gets you nowhere.

e. Politely confront your supervisor. Insist that he give you specific written feedback about your performance. (4)

This can be a productive approach, depending on the nature of your relationship with the supervisor. However, going to human resources may work better. If the problem is with your supervisor, it may serve your purpose for him to know that he is being scrutinized.

14. Domain: The Workplace

You are a <u>white employee</u> who enters the cafeteria looking for a place to sit. The only seats left are in the area where a group of black coworkers regularly sit. You feel conspicuous enough about being the only white at the table, but when you sit down, the black diners stop talking and stare at you.

What do you do?

a. Give the employees the "brother handshake." (1)

It's never a good idea to communicate with people of other racial groups with their "inside" gestures or language. Offering the "brother handshake" in this context will come off as phony and pandering.

b. Get up and change your seat. (3)

If you feel uncomfortable and see no immediate way to improve the situation, this can be a reasonable response.

c. Ignore the other people. Finish eating and leave. (2)

This is likely to exacerbate the situation, and make everyone—including you—feel more uncomfortable.

d. Confront the other employees about their rude behavior. (1)

You gain absolutely nothing by initiating a confrontation. The bad feelings you create can have ramifications that extend beyond this lunch hour.

e. Try to make light conversation with one or two people at the table. (5)

This is a smart response—one that is likely to break the ice. Using humor is an especially good idea under these circumstances. Even if the people at the table are initially uncomfortable, they are likely to loosen up if you are willing to take the lead in setting the tone.

15. Domain: Sales and Customer Service

You are a <u>*white telemarketing manager*</u> *who has recently hired a young black man whose job it is to "cold call" prospects for a home repair service. The employee is a superior salesman, but his speech is filled with "black English" expressions.*

How do you handle the situation?

a. Say nothing. (5)

A salesperson's success is based solely on his or her ability to sell. Since the young man is doing a superior job, it makes no sense to correct him.

b. Discreetly present him with a book on standard American English. (1)

This would be an especially insulting and condescending tack, and may well result in the young man's taking his talents elsewhere.

c. Gently correct his speech. (2)

Before you engage in this course of action, you need to ask yourself why. The young man's speech may make you uncomfortable. However, he's there to sell—not to reinforce your standards of proper English.

d. Have him practice with language tapes. (1)

Why would you ask a successful salesperson to waste his time with unnecessary training that he might find offensive? Your purpose as his manager is to monitor his performance, not to change his speech patterns.

e. Warn him that he must take speech training or lose his job. (1)

See the above analysis of response d.

16. Domain: Sales and Customer Service

You are a <u>white manager</u> *at a fast-food restaurant. You notice that a young white male waiter always seems to have a bad attitude toward the black and Hispanic patrons—though he is a good worker in other respects. You have spoken to him a number of times, but there has been no improvement. Waiters at this restaurant are "at will" employees. They belong to no union and can usually be fired without cause.*

What do you do?

a. Fire the waiter. (5)

Since there aren't likely to be any legal repercussions, this would be a smart response—especially since the waiter apparently hasn't responded to your previous warnings. However, "at will" employees are becoming increasingly rare, and employers normally have to go through a number of procedural steps before they let somebody go.

b. Have the waiter serve only white customers. (1)

This is an unwise course of action—one that amounts to pandering to the employee's discriminatory behavior. It would also make serving customers more cumbersome for the other waiters.

c. Send the waiter to a racial intelligence seminar. (3)

This is something employers do, either as a matter of course for all staff, or as a remedy to help a particular employee deal with a specific problem. In the case of an individual waiter, management would have to assess whether this employee is worth the investment.

d. Call a meeting of the staff and try to get to the bottom of the problem. (1)

This is an inappropriate course of action, and is likely to provoke bad feelings. The problem is with one individual—not the entire staff.

e. Assign the employee to dishwashing duty until his attitude improves. (2)

Unless this individual is a particularly good worker who you feel has the potential to change, a demotion is probably not a productive idea. The employee's continuing problems with nonwhite customers indicates a lack of motivation to act in a racially appropriate way. So, unless the demotion to dishwasher is permanent, his problems with diversity encounters are likely to resurface as soon as he is reassigned to waiting duties.

17. Domain: The Workplace

You are a <u>white manager</u> whose company has only a handful of minority employees. One of them is a Muslim, who approaches you and asks to take a day off for the celebration of Eid-El-Fitr, an important day in the celebration of Ramadan. While this is not considered an official holiday by your company, the employee points out that the plant is closed on several Jewish holidays and therefore he should have a right to take off on a day that's important to him.

What do you do?

a. Grant the request. (3)

On the surface, this would seem to be the least contentious

approach. However, you may be setting yourself up for a flood of demands to grant days off for various religious holidays. Therefore, if you are going to take this course of action, you need to carefully evaluate the potential consequences.

b. Deny the request. (1)

This response creates hostility, and may open you up to charges of discrimination. Also, if you force him to work on his holiday, the employee may not be disposed to do a very good job.

c. Tell the employee that he can leave, but he must charge it as a personal day. (5)

This is a wise policy for any company or manager to adopt. If you allow each employee a number of discretionary personal days, you will avoid debates about which holidays merit days off for which employees.

d. Explain that on the Jewish holidays in question, work is not permitted. (1)

It's not your place as a manager to interpret the meaning of specific religious holidays, or to comment on how they relate to work. Such explanations are the realm of theologians—not business-people.

e. Explain that many more employees are Jewish than Muslim. (1)

This is irrelevant. Every employee ought to be given time to worship in his or her own way—even if the individual in question is the only one in the company who practices a particular faith.

18. Domain: The Workplace

You are a <u>black high school senior</u> applying for a bank job. Your guidance counselor tells you to wear a suit and tie for the interview and to take the large earring out of your ear. Your friends say that changing your appearance makes you a sellout.

How do you handle the situation?

a. Wear the suit and tie. Tell your friends to get their acts together. (5)

If you truly want to land the job, you need to make a good impression on the interviewer. This means dressing and acting appropriately. What you tell your friends is unimportant.

b. Take out the earring, but dress the way you normally do. (1)

Halfway measures are not enough. If you want the job, go all the way. Do what needs to be done to achieve that goal.

c. Turn down the interview. (1)

An unwise strategy. What was the point of applying in the first place?

d. Refuse to sell out. Do what makes you comfortable. (1)

As we discuss in Chapter Three and elsewhere, "selling out" in this context is a misreading of the situation. If you want the job, your goal is to convince the interviewer to give it to you. If you're not interested in the position, that's another story. But remember, most corporate jobs have some kind of dress requirements, so you are effectively saying no to all of them.

e. Wear the suit and tie, but tell your friends that you agree with them, so they'll stop bugging you. (5)

Again, it doesn't matter what you tell your friends, as long as you stay focused on your goal and present yourself in a way that gives you the best chance to land the job.

19. Domain: Sales and Customer Service

You are a <u>white salesclerk</u> in a large electronics store. When a black customer asks if the price of a VCR he is considering is correct, you look at the price tag and say, "Boy! The price on that model must have just gone up."

There is a pregnant moment of silence. You realize you've accidentally said "boy," an otherwise innocuous term that you fear may have had an offensive connotation when addressing a black man.

How do you handle the situation so that the customer most likely will not walk out of the store?

a. Continue the interaction as if nothing happened. Try to be more careful in the future. (5)

This may well be the way to go, if you're relatively certain that the customer wasn't offended. If it appears that you're still going to make the sale, there's no reason to draw attention to your faux pas. The customer may not have taken offense at your words, or even noticed them. It can't do you any good to refocus his attention in that direction. Nevertheless, you would be wise to file this incident away for future reference.

b. Explain to the customer that you meant "boy" as in "oh boy!" It was not your intention to be offensive. (2)

In most cases, it's better to simply let the uncomfortable moment pass. Use this strategy only if the customer specifically states that he's taken offense at your words. In that case, it can help to use a bit of self-deprecating humor. For example, you might say, "I've been putting my foot in my mouth all day. Please excuse me." This kind of approach conveys your understanding, without making the situation worse than it is.

c. Talk about how many black friends you have. (1)

This is a very poor choice. Talking about how many black friends you have is about the same as wearing a T-shirt that says, "I am a covert racist."

d. Walk away and ask a black salesclerk to attend to this customer. (3)

This can be an acceptable backup strategy, assuming that there's a black salesclerk close by. Use it if you sense that the customer no longer wants to interact with you, and he's about to walk out of the store.

    e. Try to compensate for your faux pas by engaging the customer in small talk. (3)

This can be an acceptable approach, depending on the body language and verbal cues you receive from the customer.

20. Domain: Sales and Customer Service

You are a <u>white cab driver</u> who is new on the job. A few of the veteran cabbies have warned you to avoid black riders. A young, neatly dressed black man enters your taxi while you are standing at a red light.

What do you do?

    a. Ask him where he's going and take him there. (5)

In cities like New York, taxi drivers are legally obligated to pick up any orderly person. In theory, any stranger is capable of committing a crime, but that is one of the hazards of the job. If that danger makes you sufficiently uncomfortable, find another way to make a living.

    b. Ask him where he is going. Whatever he tells you, apologize and say that you are about to go off duty and are heading in the opposite direction. (2)

This is a tactic drivers sometimes use, simply because they don't want to go in a certain direction at the end of the day. Whatever his reason, the driver's first responsibility is to take the passenger to his destination—not to accommodate his own itinerary.

    c. Ask him where he is going. If you don't feel safe in the neighborhood he wants to go to, tell him that you are concerned about your safety. Ask if he'd consider waiting for another cab. (3)

This is a long shot that might make the passenger angry.

Nevertheless, you do have a right to consider your own safety, and there's no law against making such a request.

   d. Order him to get out of the cab. If he refuses to leave, call a cop. (1)
   This response is likely to create a lot more trouble for you than the passenger. Any cop is legally bound to order you to accommodate the passenger's request. Plus, he might decide to issue you a summons for refusing service.

   e. Ask him for payment in advance. (1)
   Any municipality that permitted such a practice would probably require a driver to obtain advance payment from all passengers, regardless of color. In addition, you have absolutely no recourse if the passenger refuses.

Please bear in mind that your RQ score measures the effectiveness of the strategies you would have selected prior to reading this book. It is not a measure of your character or prejudices. Rather than focusing solely on the numerical score, we suggest that you reflect on your responses—especially those that were ranked a 1 or 2—and consider the potential benefits of employing alternative strategies.

RAISING A RACIALLY
SMART CHILD

*To raise children who approach life with energy, optimism and self-
assurance, you must teach them how to tolerate frustration, not avoid it,
and to view adversity as a challenge—not a forerunner of failure.*

—MARTIN SELIGMAN (PSYCHOLOGIST, AUTHOR)[1]

Racial intelligence is a critical set of skills all people must have—
if they are going to succeed in an increasingly diverse environment.
Children need these skills even more, because they are starting out
in a world in which public displays of bias and ethnocentrism are
no longer acceptable.

A few of our white survey respondents commented that they
reside in homogeneous parts of the country, where they rarely
encounter a black or Hispanic. The implication is, "Why do I need
racial intelligence if I never have an opportunity to use it?" Even if
your family now lives in an all-white corner of the world, there's a
good chance that the demographics of that area will shift, or that
your child will eventually leave.

Mobility—the option to choose and drastically change one's
environment—is an ability only humans have. Business is increasingly conducted on a global basis, and this trend is likely to increase
over the coming years. Consequently, today's children are more
likely than their parents to travel and encounter people of diverse
racial and cultural backgrounds.

Anyone old enough to be a parent has seen vast changes in the racial and cultural landscape. Language and behaviors that today result in firings and multimillion-dollar lawsuits were accepted, at least tacitly, in the not-so-distant past. No more. The racial climate has shifted—and so have the demographics. Consider the following statistics:[2]

- There are currently some 62 million nonwhite people in the United States. These combined populations of blacks, Latinos, and Asian Americans grew nearly four times as fast as did the white population in the 1980s, and the trend continues.
- Minorities, who were 31 percent of the nation's children in 1990, increased to 34 percent by 2000.
- By 2010, "people of color" will account for 38 percent of the population. African Americans will account for about half of this total.
- The number of Asian Americans is projected to virtually double during that period.
- By midcentury, Latinos, the youngest and fastest-growing minority group, will constitute the largest minority population.

Perhaps more important than the raw numbers is the growing diversity among people who have influence over a young person's life and career. Today's children are far more likely to have a nonwhite teacher, visit a nonwhite physician, or wind up working for a nonwhite boss than their parents were.

Mothers and fathers who are now in their twenties, thirties, or older may have become racially smart because of their upbringing or their life experience. However, it's doubtful that their parents ever paid specific attention to how critical these skills would become in the future.

You may never have thought about it in these terms, but human beings are the only species in which each generation must teach the next generation techniques that are new and different from the ones they themselves possess. Wolves or deer, by contrast, teach their young exactly the same survival skills they learned from their parents.

Society keeps evolving, and certain competencies that were once optional are now essential. For example, many adults grew up in an era when computers were not widely used. For today's children, computer literacy has become about as important as the ability to read or add numbers.

Many of the career skills that enabled a person to make a living and negotiate the world just a generation ago are inadequate or obsolete in today's workplace. The need to help a child acquire abilities that you may not possess makes parenting an exciting challenge, but it can also create difficulties.

As we have discussed in previous chapters, people tend to be comfortable with the things they know and believe, even if they don't make sense. They tend to pass these attitudes and behaviors on to their children as if to say, "This is the way I think and act, so it must be right. I want my child to do the same."

Holding children back because of your own limitations will curtail their opportunities in the workplace, and in life. It's like denying your young son access to aspects of modern technology because they are unfamiliar to you, or refusing your daughter a college education because you don't have one.

Racial intelligence is part of the behavioral software today's children need in order to be successful. Unlike computer skills, however, no school teaches how to communicate effectively across racial lines—at least not yet. To a great extent, these are skills children either learn from their parents—or develop in spite of their parents.

If you are racially smart, your child is likely to imitate your behavior. If not, he or she will probably have to first reject your values, then go about learning how to deal with different kinds of people through a painful process of trial and error.

Parents who want their children to succeed must seek to broaden—not narrow—their horizons. That means questioning, and looking beyond, their own attitudes and values. Too many parents stunt a child's growth by trying to create miniature replicas of themselves. Fathers and mothers who impose their own biases or limited racial communication skills on children endanger their success in business and in life.

Helping a Child Understand Race and Power

Children begin perceiving colors during infancy, and soon express their color preferences in terms of clothes, toys, and other objects. Kids apply the same perceptual skills to the people they encounter. Visual cues such as hair color and skin color help a youngster figure out who's who—and it doesn't take long for kids to recognize which color differences matter most.

White children begin questioning racial differences at around age five, whereas nonwhite children can often make racial distinctions before age three. This difference in perception is not surprising, since minority children tend to be more race-conscious than their white counterparts.

Since all children want to be accepted, they are especially vulnerable to what is sometimes called the "tyranny of the majority." Much of that tyranny is more or less automatic, rather than a conscious attempt at prejudice. Most Americans are white. Therefore, whiteness is pretty much the default race—in the same way that Christianity is the default religion.

Several Jewish respondents complained about Christians who assume that everyone celebrates Christmas. "I encounter many people who aren't aware that the birth of Jesus has no meaning to those of us who aren't Christian," one Reform Jewish woman told us. "I've even been accused of being a bad mother because I don't have a Christmas tree in my house. The message is that there's something wrong or abnormal about not being part of the majority."

It's important to help children understand that other people's beliefs and practices are no less right or abnormal than their own— even if those traditions are unfamiliar. Similarly, parents need to help children recognize that no color is inherently better or more normal than any other, even if society often rewards and punishes people on this basis.

Children also need to understand the full impact of power. Children perceive who is more or less important at an early age. Those who don't belong to a group with high status or power can feel second-rate—on the outside looking in.

What happens, then, when whiteness becomes the gold standard for status and power? It certainly affects the way people see each other—as well as the way they see themselves. It influences how whites and blacks communicate, and even how some blacks deal with other blacks.

In his book, *Our Kind of People*, Lawrence Otis Graham explores America's black upper class. He notes that most of the wealthiest black families have light skin. "It started with slavery," Graham told an interviewer, "because blacks were divided into two groups of slaves.

"There were the . . . dark-skin slaves, who worked out in the fields. Then there were the [light-skinned] house slaves who had the mammies', cooks', butlers' and servants' jobs, the prestige jobs." This caste system outlasted slavery, and resulted in light-skinned former slaves being the first to get hired and educated.[3]

Graham goes on to describe what's commonly called the brown-paper-bag-and-ruler test. He observes that blacks whose skin is lighter than a brown paper bag, or whose hair is as straight as a ruler, are still given preference over those with more African features. This observation was confirmed by a number of our African American respondents.

Children, who are tremendously status conscious, will pick up these values from their parents. Before long, they begin to act on these racial perceptions. For example, several studies show that black kindergarten children will often choose white or lighter-skinned playmates, just as many black males in their teens and twenties choose to date lighter-skinned black (or white) women. The world continues to confirm the child's hypothesis: If you're white, or at least light, you're all right!

Researchers examined the influence of skin color on the earning potential of black Americans, and discovered that the relative difference in earnings between light- and dark-skinned blacks mirrors that between whites and blacks. For every 72 cents a dark-skinned black earns, a light-skinned black makes a dollar.

The researchers concluded that "blacks with the lightest skin color have the best chances for success, while those with the darkest skin color have the hardest time getting ahead."[4]

And what about whites—many of whom sit in the blazing sun and risk skin cancer trying desperately to get as dark as possible? To those whose race is the gold standard, the issue of color has a completely different connotation. If you're Caucasian, it doesn't make any difference how dark your skin is.

Peggy McIntosh, associate director of the Wellesley College Center for Research on Women, has written a controversial paper on the topic of what she calls "Whiteness Studies." In it, she describes forty-six "unearned advantages" she derives from being white.

"[If I decide to] move into new housing, I can be pretty sure that my new neighbors will be either pleasant to me or neutral. I'm never called a credit to my race. I'm never asked to speak for all people of my race.

"If I take a job with an affirmative action employer, I can be sure that my colleagues won't assume I got it because of my race, I'm keeping it because of my race, and my next promotion will be on grounds of race."[5]

McIntosh had always believed that racial bias was the product of violent or discriminatory acts by individuals. She came to realize that racism is an outgrowth of a system that bestows white people with unearned privileges from the moment they are born. This raises several questions:

- Are most white people consciously aware of the "unearned privileges" their race affords?
- If so, how do they transmit this awareness to their children?

Peggy McIntosh believes that nonwhites often make the erroneous assumption that all white people are adept at capitalizing on white privilege. She admits "[having] to do very hard work to come to see [that] doors will continue to open for us because of the history of white privilege—whether or not we intend the doors to open or whether we approve of their opening."

Ms. McIntosh's views on white privilege have more than a grain of truth. From our perspective, however, some of her ideas are the kind we've heard expressed by well-meaning white people who feel guilty, and who want to divest themselves of their unearned privilege. Not surprisingly, they want to teach their children to do the same.

As naive as they are, such notions are far less toxic than those of parents who teach their children that being white makes them better than everyone else.

Some white Americans tend to view race in much the same way that people born into wealth view material comfort. Rich people may empathize with those who are poor. They may not feel that they are any better than these individuals, and may contribute time and money to helping them. Still, we don't expect the rich to voluntarily trade places with the poor anytime soon.

Call it the luck of the draw or unearned privilege: Very few white parents are going to tell their children not to take advantage of every competitive edge they've been given. Nor should they. To encumber yourself or your child out of misplaced guilt would only serve to demonstrate both a lack of common sense—and lack of racial smarts.

Most well-meaning people value fairness, but this is a tricky issue in our culture. Children begin receiving mixed messages about fairness very early in life. Parents need to explain the difference between wishful thinking, empty rhetoric, and the way things really are.

When it comes to racial equality, there is no level playing field. Not yet, anyway. That's one reason no diversity encounter is ever completely race-neutral. Until a child understands this basic fact of life, no young person of any color can become racially smart.

• A white child who buys into the life-is-fair rhetoric will not be able to understand that people of other races often have a very different set of experiences. If life were fair, everyone would be afforded an equal opportunity to succeed, and that's not what's taking place.

• Nonwhite children need to recognize that all human beings share many of their own concerns and problems—unearned white privilege notwithstanding. People of all races and cultures generally want the same things—including good health, peace, and financial security for their families.

It's obvious to children that a person's race can account for differences in power. Nevertheless, parents need to explain that more powerful doesn't necessarily mean better. Children need age-appropriate parental guidance in order to understand how racial power politics get played out in everyday life—and in the automatic value judgments that are made about what is normal or natural.

Think about what is communicated and what is unsaid when terms like "judge," and "black judge," or "doctor," and "black doctor" are used. Lacking any information to the contrary, many people in our culture automatically assume that those in high-sounding positions are white (and male).

"Whiteness is the invisible norm," observes educational theorist Deborah Britzman, and it "colonizes the definitions of other norms [in terms of] class, gender, [and] nationality."[6] This type of categorization also masks the reality that whiteness is itself a racial category—one that comes with its own inherent problems and baggage.

Parents need to make children aware that the circumstances of one's birth create inequities between people. An individual's racial heritage always factors into the mix. Still, what counts most is helping a child develop a vision of what he or she wants to accomplish, and providing the tools that facilitate the realization of that vision.

TEACHING A CHILD TO AVOID RACE TRAPS

Because racial intelligence is an integral part of a person's operational style, and consists of diverse sorts of skills rather than one specific all-purpose method, it's not easy to teach a child to be smart in this area. Nevertheless, the effort to communicate the value—as well as the techniques—of effective racial communication is well worth the reward. The following steps will help you help your child develop a racially smart way of thinking and acting:

Be a Positive Role Model

Recent studies have emphasized the importance of peers in a child's development. In addition, the media probably have more influence today than in previous generations. Nevertheless, parents remain a child's most influential guides, in terms of teaching effective racial communication, and positive values in general.

Long before they can speak, children begin looking to their parents for messages about right and wrong. They are capable of picking up subtle cues about the way you are supposed to treat and talk to people. Answering the following questions will give you a better idea of how your behaviors may be influencing your child:

- Do you avoid expressing overt racism and reject such expressions in others?
- Do you show respect to people of different races and cultures?
- Do you exercise self-control in terms of separating emotions from behaviors?
- Do you take responsibility for your life, and expect the same of others?

If you can answer yes to these questions, you are doing your part as a role model. If you see the need to set a stronger example in one or more of these areas, we urge you to do so—for your own sake, as well as that of your children.

Talk Frankly

It's important for children to begin understanding the many ways race can influence their lives, so that they have a context for dealing with diversity encounters when they go out into the world.

We interviewed a number of middle-class black parents who intentionally insulate their youngsters from any kind of racial controversy. Some of these families live in primarily black neighborhoods (or so-called chocolate cities). To nonwhite kids who grow up in a racially cushioned environment, racial bias seems like an abstraction. However, once they go away to college or go out into the workplace, they are hit with the reality of being a minority in a white world.

Eighteen-year-old Jack grew up in one of these chocolate cities. His family and social life were almost completely localized. In many respects, he was naive about race relations and certain realities of being a black American.

For example, Jack's parents never cautioned him about racial profiling of young black male drivers by police. Jack was aware of this issue because some high-profile incidents were major news stories—but these events seemed to have nothing to do with him.

Once Jack entered college, he felt caught between two groups of students. On one side there were militant blacks, who preached racial pride and seemed to feel that all whites were racists. On the other side were white kids from affluent families, many of whom hadn't had much contact with blacks.

The local police often stopped black students as they drove around town. The first time Jack was pulled over for no apparent reason, he was surly with the police officer, who threatened to arrest him if he didn't show more respect. Jack's parents hadn't prepared him for what he was likely to encounter outside his sheltered environment. They had also shied away from discussing news events concerning racial tensions.

"I guess they were trying to protect me," Jack says now. "But I was fifteen—and felt very confused about all the racial controversy I saw on TV news shows."

We learned that Jack's mother and father had worked their way up from humble beginnings. Like many parents who were born poor, they hoped to protect their son from some of the harsher realities they had faced.

There is no question that Jack would have been better off if his parents had discussed these issues with him. As we point out in Chapter Seven, knowing how to talk to police in a racially effective way can have a huge impact on a black person's life. Furthermore, children of all races need guidance from their parents about how to interpret racially charged news events.

For example, the controversy generated by the O. J. Simpson trial gave parents an opportunity to discuss the disparity between the way blacks and whites interpreted those events. Was Simpson targeted by white racist cops because he was black? Were Simpson's lawyers right in making race a key issue in the case? Was a primarily black jury prepared to let Simpson off, whatever the evidence?

There are no simple answers to these questions. However, you can help a child by discussing the situation from a number of perspectives, not just coming down with a fixed position. Naturally, a nine-year-old won't have the same conceptual tools as a sixteen-year-old. Still, you and your child can only benefit by your presenting such issues simply, honestly, and in a way that the child understands.

Some mothers and fathers go out of their way to avoid talking about race with their children. They apparently believe that anyone who acknowledges that race matters is a racist, and that the goal is to be color-blind. Other parents are obstinate about their views, and want their children to feel and act the same as they do. Several of our respondents were so attached to their own views about race that they had a hard time even entertaining the possibility that any other perspective might be worth considering.

Parents who understand the importance of effective racial communication never try to brainwash children by instilling hatred or guilt. Nor do they avoid open discussion. Instead, they attempt to present a broad picture of race relations, while teaching and modeling some specific behavioral guidelines, including the following:

• Show respect and consideration for people of all colors and cultures. Don't participate in negative group behavior or language. If a group of kids is ridiculing or harassing others because of race, don't take part in those encounters. Don't even stand on the sidelines, because that can be taken as tacit approval.

• Don't laugh it up at someone else's expense. Racial humor is risky behavior, particularly when it's acted out in public. A white child, for example, may hear black kids calling each other the "N word" in what seems like an offhanded or funny manner. A black adolescent may overhear two Italian teens calling each other "dago." Make sure the child understands that this kind of inside banter between people of the same group is by no means an invitation for outsiders to mimic or participate.

Remember, children take many cues from their parents. If they hear you making racial jokes in a social context, they are likely to assume that this is appropriate behavior. If they hear you expressing hateful attitudes, they will assume those attitudes are correct. Certainly, you have a right to say whatever you want in the privacy of your own home. But as a parent, you need to consider the effect that exercising this freedom can have on a child.

Promote Empathy and Strength

As we have discussed, race is an important influence on a person's life-experience. There are, of course, many other significant influences, such as socioeconomic status and educational level. Still, one way or another, a person's race brings with it a particular package of likely experiences.

Children tend to be more wrapped up in their own needs and perceptions than adults. So, when a child sees someone who appears to be different, he or she is likely to frame that in terms of good or bad, better or worse. It's important to teach children to build on their own feelings and experiences by encouraging them to recognize similar feelings in others—including those who appear to be different.

Don't let your child mistake kindness and empathy for weakness. All children are vulnerable, whatever facade they may erect. Children who are unable to come to terms with their vulnerability can become bullies—and singling out someone from a minority race has long been a favorite pastime for bullies young and old.

Physically or emotionally weak kids sometimes allow themselves to be pushed around by one or more aggressive children of another racial group. It is essential to teach your child not to take on the posture of either the bully or the victim.

You don't want your children picking on others, nor do you want anyone else taking advantage of them. If your daughter or son comes home and tells you about a child of another race being mistreated, it's important to explain where this sort of behavior comes from, and then to discuss what can be done about it.

Many acts of bias are based on the fear of losing power, or of being weak and vulnerable—in short, insecure. Whether the power is economic, social, or political, emotionally insecure people often blame their own perceived deficiencies or failures on others. What can be easier than to blame your problems on an entire racial or cultural group?

Insecure people are obsessed with power, whereas those who are emotionally confident cultivate strength. Acts of bias proclaim the actor's perceived weakness or vulnerability.

Children who have the best chance of becoming racially smart are those whose parents have helped them understand that a person's most valuable resources come from within—and that successes are not defined by belittling or taking something away from others.

Children who doubt their inner strength often equate winning with disparaging others. They think, "If I put you down, I become more powerful."

Help your child identify people who use racial and cultural differences to humiliate and exert power over others. Help them understand that such people are not often very happy or successful. Contrast these individuals with men and women who have true inner strength. Use the following explanations to demonstrate that inner strength is always more desirable than power:

- Inner strength helps you to solve the toughest problems.
- Inner strength helps you to stand your ground.
- Inner strength allows you to bend without breaking.
- Inner strength causes others to perceive you as a leader.
- Inner strength helps you to think and act independently.

EIGHT STEPS TO INCREASING YOUR CHILD'S RQ

As you continue to work the eight-step process for becoming more effective in your own diversity encounters, help your children understand the principles we detail in Chapter Three. We have adapted them here for guidance on how to be a better parent:

Step 1. Recognize What You Have to Gain

Help your child recognize the benefits of becoming racially smart. Encourage the child to reflect on encounters with people of other races. Begin explaining how positive interactions can place him or her at a tremendous advantage, both now and in the years to come.

Step 2. Don't Pretend to Be Color-Blind

Help your child recognize that differences exist between people of various racial groups, based on their culture and experiences. It's not necessary for the child to understand the exact nature of those differences, but it is important for him or her to recognize the impact they can have on a person's attitudes and behavior.

Step 3. Watch, but Don't Preach

Help your child become a keen observer of racial differences without passing judgment. Encourage the child to talk honestly and openly about diversity encounters. Help him or her understand that it's okay to share feelings that might seem unacceptable—at least in the privacy of one's own home. Explain that the opinions and behaviors that result from these cultural and experiential differences don't make one person right and another person wrong.

Step 4. Build on What All of Us Share

Explain that all people are more similar than they are different. Help your child understand that most aspects of the human condition transcend race—even though that is one of the first ways we identify people who are unfamiliar. Once you get beyond race, it's easy to see that the things that make people feel happy or sad are very much the same.

Step 5. Learn from Every Experience

Help your child use each diversity encounter as an opportunity to learn about his or her mind-set, as well as that of other people.

Talk about each experience at a level the child understands. Always be honest, but don't attempt to raise questions the child doesn't broach, and may not yet be capable of understanding.

Step 6. Look at Each Situation Through the Other Person's Eyes

Explain that, although all people have much in common, a person's race and cultural background often leads to experiences that are unfamiliar to others. Help the child become watchful, without making judgments.

Explain that often, the best thing a person can do is to look, listen, and learn, without comment or action. Even if you don't understand a person's motivations, it's enough to recognize that there's usually a reason for those thoughts and actions, based on that person's experience and cultural background.

Step 7. Know What You Want to Accomplish

Show your child how to set his or her personal objective in each encounter. Stress the importance of thinking before reacting. These can be difficult tasks for children. Nevertheless, when a child discusses a diversity encounter, it's helpful to ask the following questions:

- How did it make you feel?
- How do you think the other person felt?
- What did you want to happen?
- Were you happy about what did happen?
- What would you do differently to make things go smoother?

Step 8. Close the Deal

Show your child how to generate a response that addresses the central objective in the situation—even if that objective is simply to avoid trouble.

Racially smart children develop techniques for dealing with people and situations that further their goals in ways that don't hurt others. When a young person understands what he or she is trying to accomplish in a diversity encounter, race becomes one more piece of a complex human puzzle. Racial intelligence is the key to negotiating that particular complex and fascinating component.

ELEVEN

HOW FAR HAVE YOU COME?

It is the mark of an educated mind to be able to entertain a thought without accepting it.

—ARISTOTLE

The following scenarios are based on those we use in our seminars and corporate work. Rather than score the answers as you did on the initial RQ Test, we want you to reflect on the various problem-solving approaches we present in terms of effectiveness and good sense, and think about how you might negotiate comparable situations.

1. The Crafty Manager: When to Play the Race Card

Matt, an African American, is the director of one of five sales divisions in a large multinational corporation. As part of a general retrenchment, the CEO announces that Matt's division is going to be downsized. Under the plan, Matt would retain his job and his salary, but would have far less power in the organization.

What should Matt do?
  a. Follow orders for the good of the corporation.
  b. Follow orders and start looking for another job.
  c. File a grievance with the EEOC.

    d. Slow down productivity to show what will happen if the unit is downsized.

    e. Remind the boss that he is the only African American division head in his corporation, and it might not look good to target his unit.

What happened?

Matt knew that the corporation had good reasons for its downsizing plans, and one division was going to be targeted. He genuinely believed that he was picked more by chance than for any other reason. He doubted that racism played a part. On the other hand, he had as good a claim to remain at full strength as anyone else. He gently played the race card by suggesting that if he were targeted, it might look bad for the corporation. The CEO revised his orders, and selected a different division for downsizing.

Analysis

Matt did not accuse anyone of racism. He played his cards deftly, by framing his suggestion in terms of the "good of the company." In some ways this was an elaborate bluff, and Matt would have done well to have a backup plan in reserve (perhaps starting to look for an equivalent position with another company) in case his boss called him on it. Also, this ploy can't be used too often.

Following orders without regard for the overall context is never a good idea, and many devoted employees have gotten into trouble by trusting the company too much. It was too early for Matt to look for another job, although he may have had to do so if his division was downsized. Slowing down productivity is a form of passive-aggressive behavior that is bound to backfire and alienate everyone. Filing a grievance with the EEOC with this set of facts surely would have done no good, and would have ended up labeling him as a troublemaker.

2. The Hiring Dilemma: Affirmative Action or Smart Business?

Ken is a white sales manager in a national food distributing company in a small Midwestern town with very few black employees.

Two equally qualified men—one white, one black—apply for the job of assistant sales manager.

What should Ken do?
  a. Check on his company's affirmative action policy before making a decision.
  b. Check on the state's affirmative action policy.
  c. Hire the black man.
  d. Hire the white man.
  e. Flip a coin.

What happened?

Ken hired the black applicant, who performed as well as expected, but also came up with some brand new ideas for marketing to the company's very large African American consumer base.

Analysis

Most likely, both men would have performed equally well in their sales jobs. The advantage for the manager in hiring the black applicant was much more than scoring "affirmative action points." The company is located in a geographic area with few blacks, but its national customer base is racially mixed. The new black assistant was able to bring his insights and sensitivities into sales plans to target African American customers.

Checking the affirmative action policy of the company or the state is a stilted and legalistic way to deal with a personnel problem. It's like saying, "I don't care about either the good of the company or fairness to the employees—I only care about not getting into trouble." Flipping a coin is never a good way to make a business decision.

3. Accused of Racism: Veracity versus Fear

Susan, the white thirty-nine-year-old executive director of a prestigious nonprofit organization, is having a problem with Rita, an African American senior staff member. This fifty-seven-year-old woman has complained that the organization isn't sensitive to the needs of black clients, and that she herself is being discriminated against.

Susan does not believe Rita's allegations. She has carefully looked into the claims, and has concluded that they are groundless. Susan strongly suspects that Rita is "crying racism" to cover up for her own poor job performance. Susan has considered firing Rita on several occasions, but she knows that the firing would almost certainly result in a discrimination lawsuit.

What should Susan do?
    a. Nothing.
    b. Fire Rita on the grounds of poor performance.
    c. Confront Rita and call her a bald-faced liar.
    d. Seek support from prominent African Americans, both inside and outside the organization.

What happened?

Susan was a racially intelligent manager who had developed close ties with a number of African American executives over the years. These executives knew Susan to be an unbiased person who was always fair in her treatment of staff. When Susan described her problem to these individuals, they reassured her that her instincts were correct, and gave her the support and courage to do what she believed was right.

Susan let Rita know that she had close ties with important African Americans, both in the organization and the community at large. She subsequently approached Rita and shared her true feelings about the situation. Susan then offered Rita the opportunity to take early retirement, and she accepted.

Analysis

It's not unusual for people to play the race card to get what they want—even when race is a minor or irrelevant issue. Under these circumstances, it is helpful to consult with knowledgeable people who understand the situation. Such individuals can offer mentoring, provide a sounding board, and serve as a testing ground against which you can measure your racial intelligence and sound judgment.

4. The Suspicious Stranger: Racial Profiling versus Self-Protection

Pamela, a white thirty-one-year-old newspaper editor, was coming out of a laundromat, carrying a large bag of laundry to her car. Suddenly she was approached by a black man in his twenties on a bicycle. The man came "much too close," Pamela recalls. "Close enough to bite my ear if he wanted to."

The young man never made clear what he wanted, but continued to follow Pamela to her car—never standing more than a foot away. Pamela has a brown belt in karate. She was also aware that she could use her laundry bag defensively, if that became necessary. On the other hand, she wasn't convinced that this young man was dangerous. Still, he showed no inclination to make his intentions clear, one way or the other.

What should Pamela have done?
   a. Given the man a swift karate kick and run away.
   b. Cried out for help.
   c. Talked to the man until she figured out what he wanted.
   d. Entered her car, locked all the doors and windows, and driven away.
   e. Sprayed him with mace.

What happened?
   At first, Pamela tried to talk to the man, but his strange behavior made her wary. As she approached her car, she looked the other way to divert him; then she quickly entered the vehicle, and locked the windows and doors. At this point, the young man removed a roll of bills from his pocket, and started waving them at her. Pamela was unsure if this gesture meant that he wasn't looking for money, or that he was offering to pay for sex. In any event, she drove off.

Analysis
   Pamela's response fit the circumstances. A male stranger who invades a woman's personal space without stating his intent is effectively holding up a red flag that says, "I am dangerous or mentally

unbalanced." Either way, the smartest move is to get away as quickly as possible.

Later that day, Pamela related the story to a white male friend who remarked, "It must be tough to be a black man in this society." The friend's response greatly upset Pamela. It never occurred to her that her fears and actions were the product of racial bias. Still, whatever her underlying motivations, Pamela took the smartest and safest course of action.

5. Caught Between Two Bosses: Racial Politics versus Power Politics

Lauren is a twenty-four-year-old African American marketing trainee who was assigned to work for two senior managers: Jack, a fifty-year-old African American, and Sally, a thirty-eight-year-old Japanese American. The two bosses are very different from each other, and don't get along. Jack, with only a high school education, worked his way up the corporate ladder. Sally arrived with a M.B.A., and started her career on a much higher level.

Sally continually criticizes Jack's efforts to help Lauren, and often puts him down behind his back. At one point, Sally told Lauren not to do any administrative tasks for Jack, because, technically, she is not his secretary. However, Jack has always been very nice to Lauren, and she is more than happy to do extra work for him. Sally has never done anything to help Lauren, and she becomes furious when Lauren does things for Jack. On several occasions, she has accused Lauren of favoring Jack because they are both black.

What should Lauren do?
    a. Ask for a transfer.
    b. Agree with each boss when she is with that person.
    c. Try to make peace between the two bosses.
    d. Align herself with Jack.

What happened?
Lauren always felt much more comfortable with Jack, so she decided to follow his instructions, and to let him worry about

Sally. At one point, the two bosses almost came to blows; they eventually were separated into different units. Lauren remained with Jack.

Analysis

Lauren made the smart choice; she had always felt more comfortable with Jack. She sensed that Jack liked her, in part because she was a bright young black person whom he enjoyed mentoring. Lauren recognized that Sally had no interest in her, so siding with her would have led to a career dead-end.

It is very difficult for a junior person in any organization who becomes "triangulated" between two bosses. In a sense, such a situation is like that of a child who is caught between two warring parents. A person in Lauren's position has no real power, and it would be quite grandiose to believe that she could make peace between two bosses who don't like each other. Asking for a transfer would have been an ineffective solution, especially since a far more promising option was available.

Lauren had found a mentor in Jack, and saw nothing wrong with capitalizing on his affinity for her—even if it was partially fueled by race.

6. The Uptight New Boss: Avoiding Negative Ping-Ponging

Ann, a fifty-two-year-old white engineer, had a genial relationship with the small group of colleagues with whom she had worked for the previous three years. Ann was the senior member of this work group, which consisted of eight white and Asian American engineers.

The longtime manager of this work group, who recently accepted early retirement, had a friendly and congenial personality that fit well with the other group members. Fred, a forty-six-year-old African American, was assigned to take his place.

Almost overnight, Fred's cold and distant style changed the way everybody in the group felt about coming to work. Fred seemed to bristle when others in the group joked around or made small talk. More important, Fred was the kind of boss who insisted on micro-

managing everyone's projects. This did not go over well with the group of experienced, educated professionals who were accustomed to functioning independently. Before long, what had once been a warm and trusting workplace atmosphere turned competitive and conspiratorial.

Some group members wondered if Fred's up-tightness had something to do with race. It was impossible not to notice that he was the only African American in the group. Still, Fred was highly qualified for his position, and there was no whispering about his being an affirmative action hire.

As the senior member of the group, what should Ann have done?

    a. Complained to the company president that the new manager's distant style was adversely affecting productivity.
    b. Confronted the manager and demanded that he change.
    c. Organized the rest of the staff in a campaign to unseat the new manager.
    d. Tried to understand the new manager and his sensitivities.

What happened?

Ann decided to give Fred the benefit of the doubt. Rather than taking his rigid management style as an affront, she decided that a display of caring for what might be some kind of personal insecurity could serve to loosen up this new boss.

Ann held a party at her house, and invited everyone in the group, as well as members of the support staff and several other people in the company. When Ann asked Fred to come, he said he would try. He showed up and seemed to enjoy the party. Ann was glad to see Fred engaged in friendly conversation with some of the group members and their spouses.

Later on, Ann informally suggested that other members invite Fred to join them for lunch or drinks after work. In time, Fred began to feel more a part of the group. He eventually became more relaxed, and the working atmosphere regained some of its former conviviality.

Analysis

This is a good lesson in human relationships, one that is not specifically restricted to race. When you are confronted with negativity, the reflexive response is to counter that with more negativity, thus creating a kind of adversarial game of negative ping-pong. If, however, you can find a way to counter that negativity with a demonstration of goodwill, the other person may welcome the opportunity to respond in kind.

7. The Biased Medical Director: Countering Systemic Racism

Shawna, a fifty-one-year-old black dialysis-dependent patient, feels that the caregivers at her dialysis center are not exerting a maximum effort to help the primarily black, inner-city patients. Shawna voiced these concerns to the white medical director, who assured her that he would look into the situation. However, as the director was going into his office, Shawna overheard him make the following remark to a nursing supervisor: "Those welfare people should be glad that they're getting any treatment at all."

What should Shawna do?
  a. Forget about the remark—you just can't trust white people.
  b. File a written complaint with company management.
  c. File a complaint with the state health department.
  d. Find another dialysis center.
  e. Confront the medical director, and demand an apology.

What happened?

Shawna waited until her anger subsided. An hour later, she asked the medical director to explain his remarks. As she expected, the director denied making the comment. Shawna then filed a complaint with company management, along with a petition signed by many of the other patients, demanding better medical treatment and more racial sensitivity on the part of the medical staff. Although the director continued to deny the allegations, he was reprimanded, and the services improved.

Analysis

Overt racism should never be ignored in any setting—and certainly not in one involving health. Almost everyone understands that "those welfare people" is a thinly disguised code phrase for "those damned black people." No environment is bias-free, and people who make racist remarks will rarely admit them. Therefore, targets of racism should seek the intervention of the appropriate higher authorities, especially when such intervention is likely to further their goals.

In this scenario, Shawna had the support of other patients, and made a correct assessment that company management would not want to risk bad publicity or a boycott or a medical malpractice lawsuit.

8. A Child's Questionable Color: Responding to Accidental Racism

Jennifer, a forty-six-year-old white Jewish homemaker, attempted to register her adopted Asian American daughter at the local Hebrew school. When the principal saw that the child wasn't white, she asked to see papers proving that the girl had been converted to Judaism. At the same time, there were several white adopted children who were also registering. However, their parents were not asked to present similar proof.

What should Jennifer have done?
  a. Confronted the principal—this was obviously racism.
  b. Forgotten about the incident, because any complaint might be held against the child.
  c. Found another school.
  d. Held any critical comments until the child was out of the school, but carefully monitored the situation for other signs of bias.

What happened?

Jennifer presented the conversion papers, and the child was registered in the class. However, her husband, Stu, was upset. He felt that by asking only the nonwhite child for proof that she belonged, the principal was engaging in a form of race discrimination. The principal should either take the parents' word or ask all children to present similar proof.

Stu wanted to express his feelings to the principal, so that the school would commit to a more evenhanded policy. However, Jennifer implored him not to do so, to avoid stigmatizing the child; and her husband eventually relented.

Analysis

The principal is an accidental—perhaps a covert—racist. She probably is not fully aware that her request was discriminatory—and she will probably continue to single out nonwhite children in this way.

In retrospect, Jennifer wishes she had said something to the principal, even though the child has continued to attend the school and there has been no further incident. Still, Jennifer now agrees with her husband that a religious institution ought to make a special effort to avoid all appearances of racism.

9. The Cultural Sellout: Buffer-Zone Activation

Angela Hernandez, a thirty-five-year-old drug counselor, was criticized by a Hispanic patient while leading a group therapy session. "You've got a Spanish name, but come off like a white broad who is ashamed of her heritage," the patient shouted. "You look white, walk white, talk white!"

Angela felt very uncomfortable, because the patient had hit a nerve. Angela has a Latin-sounding surname and is of Mexican descent, but she looks Caucasian. She was raised in a predominantly white community, by a family who placed no special emphasis on their Mexican heritage and culture. "Considering my family background and college education, it's embarrassing to admit that I'm not fluent in Spanish," Angela explained. "Despite all that, I do have strong feelings for people who share my heritage."

What should Angela have done?
    a. Ignored the patient's remarks and moved on with the session.

    b. Asked the patient if he would like to be switched to a group led by another counselor.

    c. Confronted the patient's anger. Told him that his remarks were completely out of line.

    d. Tried to empathize with the patient's feelings, and moved forward with the counseling session.

What happened?

Instead of responding with defensive anger, Angela smiled at the man and said, "I know looks can be deceiving, but how about giving this *wannabe muchacha* a break?" At that point, the patient stopped his attack. By being self-deprecating and using a Spanish word or two, Angela was able to deflect the patient's criticism and ease the resulting tension.

Analysis

Angela responded in a professional and racially intelligent manner by empathizing with the patient's feelings and not putting him down. By employing humor, she allowed herself and the patient to pull back from their strong feelings. Instead of becoming defensive, Angela took a moment to create a buffer zone between her self-protecting emotions and a too-quick response that could have impeded her effectiveness as a counselor.

This scenario also demonstrates the strong feelings that can be generated by using external attributes like appearance or surname as a pretense for playing out stereotypes. The key to Angela's success in this negotiation was having the strength and intelligence to address her client's sense of betrayal—rather than interpret it as an assault on her ego.

10. The Unfamiliar Roommate: Overcoming Racial Stereotypes

Clara, a forty-one-year-old African American, has been assigned to share a room with a white female on an important business trip. Clara is very apprehensive. She has worked with whites, but has never shared a room with one. She recalls a friend once telling her that whites "give off a funny smell." Clara doesn't know if this is true, but she tried hard to change her room assignment. However, she was not successful.

What should Clara do?
   a. Grudgingly accept the assignment, but have nothing to do with the white roommate.
   b. Accept the assignment. Attempt to bridge the racial divide with the roommate.
   c. Call in sick and stay home.
   d. Seek counseling to better understand her insecurities.

What happened?

Clara decided to go on the trip. When her white roommate arrived, Clara was already in bed. After introducing herself, Clara asked the roommate if she slept with rollers in her hair. This light-hearted remark broke the ice, and all of Clara's fears were soon put to rest. The two women got along well—and there were no unusual incidents or smells.

Analysis

Race should never stand in the way of efficiency and productivity in a business context. People tend to be frightened by the unfamiliar, and can have exaggerated fantasies of how uncomfortable they're going to be. The reality is never as bad as the fantasy in such a benign encounter. Once they actually roomed together for the night, the two women had no problem getting along.

Epilogue

THE QUEST CONTINUES

This book has been a journey through largely uncharted territory, which we continue to explore. We are pleased that you have taken time to join us, and hope that you consider the time well spent.

We had a singular mission in writing this book: to help you get what you want and to stay out of trouble when interacting with people of different racial groups. The best way to achieve that is by developing effective strategies through intelligent reflection on your own experiences—as well as thinking about the real-life scenarios that appear throughout the chapters.

We urge you to use the principles in this book to become smarter and more successful in your dealings across racial lines. Whenever you reach an impasse in a diversity encounter or find yourself confused by the way others act and talk, use this book as a resource and a testing ground.

Our research in the field of effective racial communication is ongoing—as is our commitment to helping individuals and organizations navigate this always-interesting and sometimes-treacherous terrain.

We invite you to share your experiences, comments, and questions with us. If you would like to join the dialogue, or want updated information about our seminars and workshops, please visit our website: www.racetrap.com.

Notes

CHAPTER ONE

1. Hubert Humphrey is quoted in Richard B. Kahlenberg, "The Practice: Did a Law Firm Mistreat One of Its Senior Associates Because He Was Black?" *New York Times Book Review*, January 3, 1999.
2. Lawrence Mungin's story is detailed in Paul B. Barret, *The Good Black: A True Story of Race in America* (New York: Dutton, 1999).
3. Rosabeth Moss Kantor is quoted from her Foreword to Lawrence Otis Graham, *The Best Companies for Minorities* (New York: Plume, 1993).
4. George Davis, "Cultural Diversity and Corporate America." *Black Collegian*, March/April 1994.
5. Michele Galen, "White, Male, and Worried." *Business Week*, January 31, 1994.

CHAPTER THREE

1. Bruce A. Jacobs, *Race Manners: Navigating the Minefield Between Black and White Americans* (New York: Arcade, 1999).
2. The case of British nanny Louise Woodward was widely reported. Sources include "Woodward Case Was Tried Again in the Court of Public Opinion." *Minneapolis Star Tribune*, November 11, 1997.
3. The incident at Bloomingdale's was depicted on "Under Suspicion." ABC *20/20*, February 27, 1998.

CHAPTER FOUR

1. William Bennett Turner, "Don't Say That at Work." *San Francisco Chronicle*, May 28, 1999.

2. The Texaco tape story was widely reported. Sources include Linn Washington, Jr., "Racism at Texaco—Not New and Not Isolated: Glass Ceiling Remains." *Philadelphia Tribune*, November 29, 1996.

3. Fuzzy Zoeller's remarks, and the observation that "others would have loved to say what he said," are from Michael Wilbon, "Zoeller's Comments Expose Need for Racial Tolerance" (Commentary). *Minneapolis Star Tribune*, May 1, 1997.

4. Jimmy the Greek's remarks are recounted in Syl Jones, "If Reggie White Can Face Music, Why Can't Gang at KQ?" *Minneapolis Star Tribune*, April 10, 1998.

5. Francis Lawrence's unfortunate language is recounted in Mike Lupica, "Campanis Was a Victim." *Newsday*, February 12, 1995.

6. Fred Goodwin's comments are recounted in Linda Douglas, "Is Violence a Public Health Issue? Question Provokes Fierce Debate." *Black Issues in Higher Education*, December 15, 1994.

7. Al Campanis's original comments on *Nightline* were recounted on "Baseball in Black and White." ABC *Nightline*, April 11, 1997.

8. Campanis's comment, "People only heard that one thing from me. Then they never wanted to listen to me again," is quoted in Lupica, "Campanis Was a Victim."

9. The "niggardly" incident was described in Jonathan Yardley, "Use the Right Word for the Times." *Washington Post*, February 1, 1999.

10. Benjamin Franklin's use of "niggardly" was cited in Yardley, "Use the Right Word for the Times."

11. Reference to a "thought police" culture is cited in Rachel Sylvester and Colin Blackstock, "Straw Says Race Report Goes Too Far." *Independent on Sunday*, February 28, 1999.

CHAPTER FIVE

1. Rosabeth Moss Kantor, from her foreword to Lawrence Otis Graham, *The Best Companies for Minorities* (New York: Plume, 1993).

2. Carolyn Corbin, *Conquering Corporate Codependence: Lifeskills for Making It Within or Without the Corporation* (New York: Prentice-Hall, 1993).

3. The allegations of discrimination at Wonder Bread are detailed in "Blacks Threaten to Boycott." *Sun Reporter*, November 26, 1998.

4. Franklin Templeton, "In Wake of Bias Lawsuit, Coca-Cola Establishes Racial Diversity Council." *Los Angeles Times*, May 27, 1999.

5. Jack Welch is quoted in Noel M. Tichy and Sherman Stradford, *Control Your Destiny or Someone Else Will* (New York: Doubleday, 1993).

6. David Segal, "Denny's Touts Turnaround from Chain's Racial Black Eye: Restaurants Begin Drive to Woo Back Minority Customers." *Washington Post*, April 11, 1999.

7. Jenny C. McCune, "Diversity Training: A Competitive Weapon." *Management Review,* June 1, 1996.

8. Texaco's Peter Bijur is quoted from Kurt Eichenwald, "Texaco Acts Against Execs in Bias Case: One Dismissed, One Suspended; Two Retirees Lose Benefits." *Dallas Morning News*, January 9, 1997.

9. Texaco becomes "a beacon of light." Peter Bijur's statement is quoted in Carl Weiser, "Texaco Race-Discrimination Case Settled for $176.1 Million." Gannett News Service, November 15, 1996.

10. Texaco's turnaround and the accompanying skepticism are detailed in Kenneth Labich, "No More Crude at Texaco." *Fortune*, September 6, 1999.

11. Paraphrased from John Steinbeck, *The Grapes of Wrath* (New York: Penguin USA, 1992 reissue edition).

12. The *Nappy Hair* story is recounted in James Ahearn, "A Sad, Predictable Story." *Bergen Record*, December 6, 1998.

13. Insurance companies' advice on avoiding discrimination lawsuits is detailed in Rebecca Piirto Heath, "The Dispute-Free Workplace: Business Insurance Must Protect Against Lawsuits, Too." *Business Journal*, May 3, 1999.

CHAPTER SIX

1. Quote by Amy Hilliard-Jones is from Janean Chun, "Direct Hit: Want to Hit a Marketing Bull's-Eye? Set Your Sights on a Smaller Target." *Entrepreneur,* October 1, 1996.

2. John Romandetti is cited in David Segal, "Denny's Touts Turnaround from Chain's Racial Black Eye: Restaurants Begin Drive to Woo Back Minority Customers." *Washington Post,* April 11, 1999.

3. Denny's chief diversity officer cited in Segal, "Denny's Touts Turnaround."

4. Statistics documenting Denny's turnaround are cited in Segal, "Denny's Touts Turnaround."

5. The importance of moments of truth in customer service is detailed in Jan Carlzon, *Moments of Truth* (New York: HarperCollins, 1989).

6. "Muslims Sue Denny's Over Pork Incident." *Newsday,* January 21, 1999.

7. The incident at Denny's involving a group of thirty black middle school students is reported in "Discrimination Suit Filed Against Denny's: Troubled Restaurant Chain Will Contest the Lawsuit." Associated Press, June 8, 1999.

8. Joe Girard is quoted from a coauthor interview.

9. Research revealing that many African American salespeople are "acutely conscious of stereotypic thinking" is cited in J.A.F. Nicholls and Leslie Vermillion, "Diversity in the Sales Force: Problems and Challenges." *Journal of Personal Selling and Selling Management,* fall 1998.

10. Statistics regarding differences between racial and ethnic groups in terms of body language and the need for personal space are cited in Kate Halpern, "The Postures That Speak Louder Than Words." *Independent,* January 29, 1998.

11. Jo-Ellan Dimitrius's description of different kinds of liars is cited in Janice Turner, "Getting a Read on Friend or Foe." *Toronto Star,* July 13, 1998. Other relevant material on this topic appears in her cowritten book: Jo-Ellan Dimitrius and Mark Mazzarella, *Reading People: How to Understand People and Predict Their Behavior, Anytime, Anyplace* (New York: Ballantine, 1999).

12. Principles of win-win negotiations are detailed in Roger Fisher and William Ury, *Getting to Yes: Negotiating Agreement Without Giving In* (New York: Penguin Books, 1983).

13. Source for market research statistics: Ogilvy Adams & Rinehart, Washington, D.C., as cited in "Advertising's Changing Face: Multicultural Markets Require Audience-Specific Advertising." *Florist,* January 1996.

CHAPTER SEVEN

1. The incident in which two New Jersey state troopers shot into a van is detailed in Seamus McGraw, "Turnpike Shooting." *Bergen Record,* April 25, 1998.

2. David A. Harris, "Driving While Black: Racial Profiling on Our Nation's Highways." An American Civil Liberties Union Special Report, University of Toledo College of Law, June 1999 (Issued by the ACLU).

3. Colonel Williams's diatribe is cited in Jerry Seper, "Arrest Records Back Comments of Fired Chief; N.J.'s Top Trooper Linked Drugs to Race." *Washington Times,* March 2, 1999.

4. Whitman's remarks concerning Williams are detailed in Jerry Seper, "Whitman: Fired Top Cop Not Racist, But Insensitive." *Washington Times,* March 4, 1999.

5. Clinton's approval of profiling of Hispanics is detailed in Jerry Seper, "Clinton Supported Racial Profiling in Arkansas; Now Calls Practice 'Morally Indefensible.'" *Washington Times,* June 21, 1999.

6. Christopher Darden is quoted from "America in Black and White— Fitting the Profile." ABC *Nightline,* March 31, 1998.

7. California Assemblyman Chris Tucker's remark is quoted from "Police Brutality! Four Los Angeles Officers Are Arrested for a Vicious Beating, and the Country Plunges into a Debate on the Rise of Complaints Against Cops." *Time,* March 2, 1991.

8. Dr. Beverly Anderson is quoted from a coauthor interview.

9. The *Washington Post* report on gun discharge in various cities is cited in John Riley, "Race and Deadly Force/Cops, Civil Rights:

Shootings Ignite a National Debate." *Newsday,* March 14, 1999.

10. Statistics on citizen complaints against police are cited in Riley, "Race and Deadly Force."

11. Michelle van Ryn is quoted from Ford Fessenden, "The Health Divide: A Difference of Life and Death." *Newsday,* November 29, 1998.

12. The study by the independent Institute of Medicine is cited in Sheryl Gaye Stolberg, "Do No Harm: Breaking Down Medicine's Culture of Silence." *New York Times,* December 5, 1999.

13. Dr. Lucian Leape is quoted from Stolberg, "Do No Harm."

14. An important source of information on the racial disparity in medical care is the series "The Health Divide: A Difference of Life and Death." *Newsday,* November 29–December 5, 1998.

15. The *New England Journal of Medicine* revealing that doctors were 40 percent less likely to order sophisticated cardiac tests for blacks is cited in Kirk A. Johnson, "The Color of Health Care." *Heart and Soul,* March 31, 1994.

16. The difference in the way black and white diabetes patients are treated is detailed in Ford Fessenden, "The Health Divide: A Difference of Life and Death/For Blacks, Medical Care and State of Health Trail Whites." *Newsday,* November 29, 1998.

17. Sources of information on the achievement gap include Michael Markowitz, "The Achievement Gap—Teaneck Is Pressed to Narrow Disparities in Performance Between Whites, Minorities." *Bergen Record,* April 9, 1995.

18. The discussion on dealing with the educational system draws on material from Muriel Karlin Trachman and Gene Busnar, *Raising a Successful, Happy Child,* an unpublished manuscript.

19. Brent Staples's story about the teacher who inspired him can be found in his book *Parallel Time* (New York: Panthcon Books, 1994).

20. The quota against Asian American students is detailed in Paul Van Slambrouck, "College Acceptance Season: Asian Students Struggle with High Rate of Success." *Christian Science Monitor,* March 18, 1999.

CHAPTER EIGHT

1. Booker T. Washington, *Up From Slavery* (Phoenix: Dover, 1995).
2. Jesse Jackson's remark is quoted in Rupert Cornwell, "Out of America." *Independent,* January 12, 1994.
3. Brent Staples describes his anger at being profiled in *Parallel Time* (New York: Pantheon Books, 1994).
4. Gavin De Becker, *The Gift of Fear: Survival Signals that Protect Us from Violence* (New York: Dell, 1999).
5. Sidebar statistics cited in Gavin De Becker, "Fear, What Americans Are Afraid of Today: Conquering What Scares Us." *USA Weekend,* August 24, 1997.
6. Lawrence Otis Graham details his restaurant experiences in *Member of the Club: Reflections on Life in a Racially Polarized World* (New York: HarperPerennial Library, 1996).
7. Douglas Wilder's degrading encounter at the Raleigh-Durham airport is detailed in Hans J. Massaquoi, "The New Racism: No Matter How High They Climb on the Ladder of Success, Black VIPs Say They Are Far from Immune to Bigotry." *Ebony,* August 1996.

CHAPTER TEN

1. Martin Seligman, *Learned Optimism* (New York: Alfred A. Knopf, 1991).
2. Demographic statistics are from the United States Census Bureau.
3. Lawrence Otis Graham, *Our Kind of People: Inside America's Black Upper Class* (New York: HarperCollins, 1999).
4. Research on the influence of skin color on earning potential is detailed in Kathy Y. Russell, Midge Wilson, and Ronald E. Hall, *The Color Complex* (New York: Harcourt Brace and Company, 1992).
5. Peggy McIntosh's "white privileges" are quoted from Jeb Sharpe and Robert Siegel, "Whiteness Studies." *All Things Considered,* National Public Radio, January 2, 1998.
6. Deborah Britzman is cited in "Lady Bountiful: The White Woman Teacher in Multicultural Education." *Women's Education/Education des femmes,* September 1, 1994.

INDEX

diversity encounters *(continued)*
  stereotypical crime fears in,
    148–55
  tension in, 102–3
  white fear vs. black anger in,
    147–52
diversity training, 93, 94–95
doctoral degrees, 157
drugs, 118, 119, 131

educational systems, 138–43
  achievement levels in, 57–58,
    138–39
  cheating in, 23, 85–86,
    174–75
  college admissions and, 22,
    141, 142–43, 172–73
  curriculum choices in, 80–83
  parental involvement in, 113,
    114, 140–42
EEOC (Equal Employment
    Opportunity Commission),
    75, 205, 206
Eid-El-Fitr, 27, 183
elevator encounters, 20, 167–70
emotions, actions disconnected
    from, 74, 78–80, 86, 122,
    150, 216
employees
  after-hours activities of, 23,
    173–74
  cafeteria seating of, 25–26,
    180–81
  civil rights protections of,
    9–10, 31, 67, 75
  cooperative relations among,
    178–79, 216–17
  in corporate downsizing,
    205–6

discrimination claims of,
    207–8
hiring of, xiii, 78–80,
    206–7
language used by, 23–24, 26,
    181–82
office politics vs. racial
    politics and, 210–11
performance evaluation of,
    84–85
personal appearance of, 7,
    27, 43–44, 184–85
promotion policies for, 25,
    179–80
racial intelligence testing of,
    73
religious holidays of, 27,
    183–84
supervisor criticisms of, 7–9,
    12–13
See also workplaces
Equal Employment Opportunity
    Commission (EEOC), 75,
    205, 206
eye contact, 106, 125

fear
  poll on objects of, 155–56
  racial stereotyping as basis
    for, 147–55, 167–70
Federal Bureau of Investigation,
    119–20
Filipina women, stereotyping of,
    53
Fisher, Roger, 109
Fourth Amendment, 117, 121
France, physical contact in,
    107
Franklin, Benjamin, 60

Fuller, Laurance, 14

genetics, racial myths about,
56–58
Getting to Yes (Fisher and Ury),
109
Gift of Fear, The (De Becker),
155
Girard, Joe, 96–97
globalization, trends in, 189
Goodwin, Fred, 58
Graham, Lawrence Otis,
159–60, 193
Grapes of Wrath, The
(Steinbeck), 74
Great Britain, physical contact
in, 107

health care system, 114
black doctors in, 21–22,
137–38
black patients in, 129–36,
213–14
"hardiness" stereotype and,
130–31
impersonal behavior in, 91,
129–30, 131, 134
physician mistakes and, 130,
135
health maintenance organizations
(HMOs), 21–22, 133–34,
137–38, 170
heart disease, 133
Hernandez, Angela, 215–16
high blood pressure, 135
Hilliard-Jones, Amy, 89
Hindus, 111
hiring policies, 78–80
racial preferences in, xiii, 206–7

Hispanics
cultural identity of, 215–16
education of, 139
language of, 56, 126
market research on, 111
physical contact among, 107
police relations with, 114,
116–21
population levels of, 190
HMOs. *See* health maintenance
organizations
holidays, religious, 27, 36, 71,
183–84, 192
housing, equal rights to, 146
Howard, David, 60
Hubbard, Elbert, 1
humor, 22, 82, 171–72,
199–200
Humphrey, Hubert H., 9
hypertension, 135

inner strength, power vs., 201
intelligence, 13, 16, 57–58, 131

Jackson, Jesse, 148
Jacobs, Bruce, 29
Japan, U.S. business rivalry
with, 59
Jews
Christmas and, 192
dietary restrictions of, 111
inside humor among, 82, 200
religious holidays of, 27, 183,
184
social stereotypes of, 53
job interviews, 112
background checks and, 115
personal appearance in, 7, 27,
43–44, 184–85